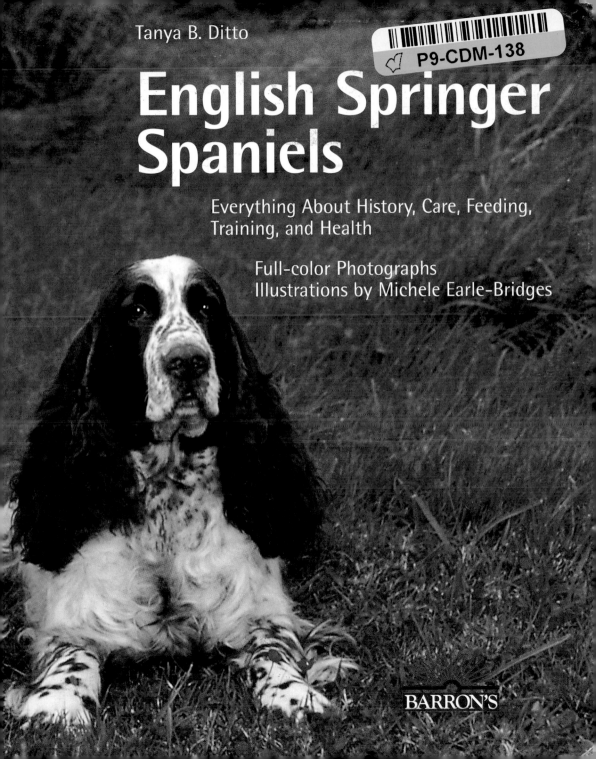

Tanya B. Ditto

English Springer Spaniels

Everything About History, Care, Feeding, Training, and Health

Full-color Photographs
Illustrations by Michele Earle-Bridges

BARRON'S

CONTENTS

HISTORY OF THE SPRINGER SPANIEL

The spaniel, its ancestry buried in the mist of history, is often called the "Adam" of the dog world. Geoffrey Chaucer, a fourteenth-century storyteller, referred to a "spaynel" dog that liked to "lepe" at people. Our Springer, perhaps?

Owners praise the Springer's loyalty and devotion. Bystanders admire its magnificent coat and those long, velvet ears. Trainers appreciate its intelligence and adaptability. With so many vocal supporters on all sides, it is small wonder that Springers are among today's most sought-after breeds.

Origins and Early History

According to respected spaniel author and breed judge Maxwell Riddle, the first written reference to a spaniel occurred in Ireland in the year A.D. 17. At that time a scribe entered in the king's ledger a gift of "water spaniels." Riddle speculated that this admittedly bare reference was important beyond a simple evidence of breed existence. He pointed out that because the reference was to a specific type of spaniel,

The eyes have it.

authorities already had recognized the breed's diversity and had accepted its variances.

Archivists noted a reference to spaniels in a fifteenth-century workbook prepared by tutors for the children of King Henry IV. When the *Mayflower* arrived in America its records showed 102 passengers. Traveling with passenger John Goodman were two dogs, an English Springer Spaniel that "chased the deer," and a Mastiff. In the beginning most spaniel breeds were categorized by size and ability. Cockers, for instance, were small; Clumbers were not. Some spaniels found and pointed to the game (eventually these were known as "setters") and others, the Springers, flushed the prey from cover. Even though the springing spaniels collectively had long been known as superb gundogs and acquired the respect of bird and small game hunters, the English Springer Spaniel was recognized as a specific variety of spaniel in 1919.

The English Springer Spaniel, top dog in the home, in the show ring, and in the field.

been called by in their home country, they were inadvertently renamed by their new owners. More than likely, those who inquired about the dogs were told they hailed from Hispania, the Roman word for Spain. Thus, assorted as the dogs' physical characteristics might have been, these long-haired, for the most part flop-eared, pets were thereafter collectively referred to as "the spaniels." To this day, the spaniels they remain.

How Did the Spaniels Get Their Name?

It is generally understood and accepted by the dog "fancy" (a fancy word for those who are fond of dogs) that the early spaniels originated in Spain. What can be hard for the newcomer to understand, however, is how dogs called spaniels can be of radically diverse sizes, or sport any of several colors. Bystanders wonder at spaniels that may or may not have the typically pendulous ears, and (most importantly for a renowned hunting breed) that may exhibit no more than a passing interest in field work.

One answer lies in antiquity. Historians speculate that Roman soldiers, on their marches through the far regions of the civilized world, helped spread various spaniel-like breeds throughout Europe. It seems likely that the soldiers, undoubtedly attracted to these amiable and companionable dogs of Spain, carried the puppies from the country as pets, as souvenirs, or as helpful meat hunters. We assume that, whatever name the dogs had

The Spaniel Today

The English Springer Spaniel is one of 17 breeds of spaniels. In 2003, English Springers were listed twenty-eighth in dogdom's annual popularity contest (winners being determined by the number of dogs registered with the American Kennel Club). They are outranked in the spaniel family only by the Cocker, which is fourteenth on the list behind the number one Labrador Retrievers and second place Golden Retrievers.

Spaniel lovers recognize two distinct types and sizes of spaniels—sporting and toy. Each type evolved from deliberate and selective mating designed to accomplish a particular purpose. The dogs known as "spaniels" can properly weigh from as little as 7 pounds (3.2 kg) to a respectable 65 pounds (29.5 kg) at maturity. Some spaniels are tall and rangy; others are heavyset and short. Some are lightweight lapdogs; others are relative giants.

Coat color is an important factor in most spaniels. Even here, however, important differences mark the breeds. Breeders highly prize the reddish coat color of Welsh Springers, for instance. On the other hand, red is not an acceptable coat color for English Springers.

Although our focus is on the English Springer Spaniel, we will for a moment consider the links of kinship in the background of this remarkably diverse breed.

The Nine Sporting Spaniels

Each of the sporting spaniels, a designation given to the Springer and eight of its cousins, was bred for specific territorial needs. It would make sense that in some hunting ranges, and for some quarry, larger dogs with their greater stamina, were considered superior. The Clumbers, the largest of all spaniels, and the Sussex, one of the oldest breeds, were developed for the purpose of hunting in dense terrain. Those bird hunters who also wanted spaniels as house pets preferred smaller spaniels and in time produced a line of sturdy hunting Cockers.

English and Welsh Springers

Both the English and the Welsh Springers undoubtedly are closely related. Both are medium-sized, compact dogs, greatly admired for their hunting abilities. Both are known for their trademark trait of "springing" at game. The Welsh Springer's red and white coat is an outstanding characteristic of the breed.

Irish and American Water Spaniels

The Irish Water Spaniel is aptly named. Its love of water and its dense, oily coat, always solid liver in color, combine to produce a respected duck-hunting companion. The American Water Spaniel, a fluffier dog than the Irish Spaniel, also sports a dense, tightly curled coat.

This spaniel, developed in the United States, is thought to be a result of breedings of Irish Water Spaniels and Curly-Coated Retrievers.

American and English Cockers

Cockers were bred on both sides of the Atlantic. With the exception of bloodlines, the strains show remarkable similarity. Some historians tell us that Cockers derive their

All dressed up and ready to go.

Salilyn's "Robert."

names from their skills at hunting woodcock, a small gamebird. Others, pointing to the older use of Cocker as a word meaning to "indulge or pamper" suggest that the dog's amiable nature tempts its master to indulgence. Cockers are among the smallest of the sporting breeds, weighing at maturity about 25 pounds (11 kg).

Sussex, Field, and Clumber Spaniels

The Sussex Spaniel is one of the oldest recognized spaniels. One authority, writing in 1805, suggests that the Sussex is basically a large Cocker that was developed from strong Cocker lineage. It is only certain that this breed takes its name from Sussex, England, where it was a preferred hunting dog as long ago as the 1700s.

Field Spaniels, among the rarest of the spaniels, were apparently produced from a cross of Sussex and Cocker lines. The fields are medium-sized, solid-colored gundogs.

The massive Clumber Spaniels can properly weigh up to 65 pounds (29.5 kg). Bred to be strong gundogs able to work in dense under-

"Best in Show"

One of the premier honors in the world of dogs was bestowed on a Springer in Madison Square Garden in early February 2000. English Springer Spaniel Salilyn 'N Erin's Shameless, called Samantha, having previously won the Sporting Dog Group, was awarded Best in Show at the 124th Westminster Kennel Club Show in New York City, the judge commenting, "The Springer Spaniel, for her breed, had a slightly better head, and when you say that, you've said it all."

The honor was a family tradition. In 1967 Samantha's great-great grandfather, Ch. Salilyn's Aristocrat, was top dog at Westminster. In 1993, just seven years before her own honor, Samantha's sire, Ch. Salilyn's Condor, called Robert, won the 117th Westminster Best in Show, the only father-daughter win in the show's long history. At that time the judge said of her choice, "I was blessed with many good specimens. I think the dog that won it is a great dog. Last night was his finest hour."

brush, the Clumber is long and low to the ground. It is sometimes described as the St. Bernard of spaniels.

The Eight Toy Spaniels

In the sixteenth century, several small spaniels so amused the ladies of the English court that the breed's popularity soared. These pampered and petted lapdogs slept next to, ate at the table with, and went riding alongside their mistresses. Rarely did the ladies allow

English and Welsh Springers differ in size, shape, and color.

their pets the run of the halls for fear of their being trampled, or worse, set upon by larger dogs. It became a habit for their mistresses to carry around these small, warm "comforter" spaniels nestled in a stomach snuggler, much the same carrier as is used for babies today. The practice also provided a little warmth for the ladies on chilly winter mornings.

The spaniel was such a hit in England that by the seventeenth century an assortment of spaniels accompanied King Charles II through the halls of his palaces. It is said that Charles, known as the Merry Monarch, not only allowed his dogs into his council meetings, but permitted his favorites to have their puppies in his bedroom.

The sporting instinct in the toy spaniels remains high. But, don't be misled by the word spaniel in their breed name and expect the toys to be active outdoor hunting dogs, albeit smaller. They are not. The toys love water and the outdoors as much as their larger cousins, the sporting spaniels do, but toys cannot handle much of either. Although the toys do retain much of their hunting instinct, and enjoy a bout with backyard squirrels and rabbits, for example, they are neither temperamentally nor physically suited for true hunting. These are tiny, sensitive bundles of energy that much prefer a chase through your pockets in search of a bit of cheese.

English Toy Spaniels

Although their origin is undoubtedly Japanese, these bright-eyed so-called sleeve, or lapdogs, have been known and loved in England and Scotland since the sixteenth century. Favored with blunt, upturned muzzles, the English Toy Spaniels gaze appealingly upward.

Their typically large, black eyes and enormous pupils focus intently on their patrons. Bright and energetic, the English Toy Spaniels enjoy a pampered lifestyle and, in return, live up to their reputation as pleasant companions.

All five of the English spaniels mentioned next are closely related. Color variation is usually the key to identification.

King Charles and Ruby English Spaniels: The early spaniels favored by the seventeenth-century Merry Monarch, and those that eventually received his name, were black and tan. Apparently several coat color mutations occurred through the years that eventually brought about the five varieties known today. Today, breed guidelines consider this black-and-tan dog a "solid" color because the mahogany tan coloration is limited to the muzzle, chest, and legs with some tan coloration over the prominent eyes.

What do you want to be when you grow up?

The Ruby Spaniel, a rich chestnut red, is a solid color dog, with no markings. The Ruby Spaniel has a beautiful head, and like the other toys, sports long, ruffly feathered ears that occasionally reach 20 inches (51 cm) in length.

Blenheim and Prince Charles English Spaniels: It is said that the original breeding pair of what came to be known as Blenheims was a set of red-and-white Cockers brought to England from China. Their coats are considered "broken-colored" (as opposed to the King Charles and the Ruby Spaniels, which are whole-colored). Both the Blenheim and the King Charles display an overlay of patches, either bright red chestnut or ruby-red, on a pearly white background. One distinctive and identifying feature of the Blenheim is a dime-sized spot of red at the top of its forehead.

The Prince Charles English Spaniel is a tri-colored dog of white, black, and tan. As in the Blenheims, the predominant color is usually pearly white, with the black scattered in patches. As in the King Charles, the tan is limited to an area above the eyes, on the muzzle, chest, and legs. One major distinction between the Prince Charles and the Blenheim is that the Prince Charles has no spot on its forehead.

Cavalier King Charles English Spaniels: The background coat color on the Cavalier can be a solid shiny red or a solid pearly white, but all Cavalier coats have markings of chestnut, black, or tan. Like the other toys, these pets are loving, affectionate, and perfectly suited for small living quarters.

Japanese Spaniel

Like its toy cousins, the Japanese Spaniel (known also as the Japanese Chin) is an aristo-cratic oriental-looking dog, usually black and

I want to look just like them.

white. The Chin's alert eyes are large and prominent. Its plumed tail, which is a distinctive feature of the breed, is carried high. Introduced to the West in 1853 by Commodore Perry, who presented several to Queen Victoria as gifts from the Emperor of Japan, the Chins have a stylish look about them that enhances their popularity.

Tibetan Spaniel

For centuries inhabitants of the isolated, mountainous country of Tibet had little contact with the outside world. When visitors did arrive, however, they were usually offered the hospitality of the monasteries and palaces. Following these visits the newcomers wrote admiringly of the catlike little spaniels of Tibet.

The history of the Tibetan Spaniel is steeped in symbolism. In memory of the teachings of the Lord Buddha, who had tamed the lion to follow at his heels "like a faithful dog," the Tibetans referred to their loyal spaniels as "little lions."

Hence the term "lion dog" has accompanied the breed to this day. On their departure the visitors were occasionally presented with these

SPRINGER SOUNDBITES

"The gift which I am sending you is called a dog, and is in fact the most precious and valuable possession of mankind."
Theorodus Gaza

The frost is in the air.

affectionate, light-eyed spaniels as symbols of peace and friendship.

Papillon

The Papillon, or Continental Toy Spaniel, does not have the hanging ears typical of the spaniel family; instead, its erect, feathered ears are held upright. When in motion, the ears remind the observer of the spread wings of a butterfly, hence its name. (*Papillon* means "butterfly" in French.) This well-liked little spaniel is thought to be a descendant of the fifteenth-century spaniels seen in paintings on museum walls

today. These pampered pets are often portrayed nestled in the laps or at the feet of their rich and famous owners as they obediently posed for the portraits that we still admire.

The Springer: Top Dog

The English Springer Spaniel, as we have seen, has 16 first cousins, and each breed has its own cheerleaders. If you would like to pursue your interest, breed clubs will share their information. Newcomers are always welcome at club gatherings and shows. Any of the breed

Waiting for the call.

clubs can be contacted for literature and for information. Addresses can be obtained from the American Kennel Club (see Information, page 92).

The Springer, however, which is top dog in this book, has its own cheerleaders in some pretty fancy places. Want a dog that can write a bestseller? One Springer did just that when Millie, "The White House Dog," coauthored a memoir with the help of her owner, former First Lady Barbara Bush. Proceeds from the First Dog's unabashedly immodest account are donated to the Barbara Bush Foundation for Family Literacy.

Perhaps you already own a Springer. Maybe you still are considering a purchase. This book is designed to help you make the right decisions as you travel the long road of friendship together. Keep the book handy and refer to it when you have a question. Be observant. Have fun. Have confidence that as you and your Springer take those first steps of companionship and friendship together, your own finest hours lie ahead.

UNDERSTANDING SPRINGER SPANIELS

The typical Springer is friendly, loyal, eager to please, quick to learn, and willing to obey. An all-around companion, the Springer has a competitive spirit capable of earning honors in the field, in the show ring, and in your heart.

Understanding Dogs

Eons ago, humans and dogs embarked upon a mutually beneficial journey that culminated in a centuries-long friendship. That friendship was forged with trust, sharing, and an endless ability to forgive.

Writers through the ages composed poems, essays, speeches, and epitaphs honoring their faithful friends that had passed on. Although this praise and respect, often honoring the dog's unconditional loyalty and steadfast courage, comes to all breeds, that for the spaniel is unsurpassed.

Humanity's Helper

The dog has assisted humans in numerous ways through the centuries of their friendship. From the beginning, man and dog hunted

Ready to go, rain or shine.

together to provide food for the family. If an arrow missed its mark, the dog retrieved the arrow. If the arrow hit or wounded its target, the dog retrieved the game.

In the intervening centuries, dogs have learned to carry messages, to guard property, to search debris for victims, and to play the circus clown. Today, dogs perform services for disabled people, enabling many to lead productive and independent lives. Many dogs are part of therapy groups visiting hospitals and nursing homes as part of a nationwide program reaching out to shut-ins.

Understanding Your Springer

The English Springer Spaniel is an alert, intelligent dog deserving of the title all-around companion. Few spaniels can top the English Springer's superior athletic ability. A respected

At the beach.

hunting dog, a bird hunter with few equals, the Springer has a competitive spirit capable of earning honors in the field, in the show ring, and in your heart.

External Appearance

The first thing most people notice about a Springer is the beautiful, pendulous ears well covered with fine feathered hair. In addition to their handsome appearance, the ears, set at about eye level, also perform the functional service of protecting the dog's external ear canal from inflammation.

✔ A Springer is bred with a good, heavy muzzle, and long, muscular neck, specifically intended to help him retrieve game. Hunters like to say that "A Springer grasps with the teeth but weight is borne by the neck."

✔ The Springer coat is of many colors, dense enough to be waterproof and thornproof, but light enough to be glossy and refined in texture.

✔ Its overall appearance should give the onlooker an instant impression of the grace and stamina of the breed.

The English Springer Spaniel Field Trial Association (ESSFTA) writes and the American Kennel Club (AKC) endorses a breed Standard that serves as a guideline for breeders and judges.

English Springer Spaniel Standard

General Appearance: The English Springer Spaniel is a medium-sized sporting dog with a compact body and a docked tail. His coat is moderately long, with feathering on his legs, ears, chest and brisket. His pendulous ears, soft gentle expression, sturdy build and friendly wagging tail proclaim him unmistakably a member of the ancient family of Spaniels. He is above all a well-proportioned dog, free from exaggeration, nicely balanced in every part. His carriage is proud and upstanding, body deep, legs strong and muscular, with enough length to carry him with ease. Taken as a whole, the English Springer Spaniel suggests power, endurance and agility. He looks the part of a dog that can go, and keep going, under difficult hunting conditions. At his best he is endowed with style, symmetry, balance and enthusiasm, and is every inch a sporting dog of distinct character, combining beauty and utility.

Size, Proportion, Substance: The Springer is built to cover rough ground with agility and reasonable speed. His structure suggests the capacity for endurance. He is to be kept to medium size. Ideal height at the shoulder for dogs is 20 inches, for bitches, it is 19 inches. Those more than one inch over or under the breed ideal are to be faulted. A 20 inch dog, well-proportioned and in good condition, will weigh approximately 50 pounds; a 19 inch bitch will weigh approximately 40 pounds. The length of the body (measured from point of shoulder to point of buttocks) is slightly greater than the height at the withers. The dog too long in body, especially when long in the loin, tires easily and lacks the compact outline characteristic of the breed. A dog too short in body for the length of its legs, a condition which destroys balance and restricts gait, is equally undesirable. A Springer with correct substance appears well-knit and sturdy with good bone; however, he is never coarse or ponderous.

Head: The head is impressive without being heavy. Its beauty lies in a combination of strength and refinement. It is important that its size and proportion be in balance with the rest of the dog. Viewed in profile, the head appears approximately the same length as the neck and blends with the body in substance. The stop, eyebrows and chiseling of the bony structure around the eye sockets contribute to the Springer's beautiful and characteristic expression, which is alert, kindly and trusting. The **eyes**, more than any other feature, are the essence of the Springer's appeal. Correct size, shape, placement and color influence expression and attractiveness. The eyes are of medium size and oval in shape, set rather well-apart and fairly deep in their sockets. The color of iris harmonizes with the color of the coat, preferably dark hazel in the liver and white

dogs and black or deep brown in the black and white dogs. Eyerims are fully pigmented and match the coat in color. Lids are tight with little or no haw showing. Eyes that are small, round or protruding, as well as eyes that are yellow or brassy in color, are highly undesirable. **Ears** are long and fairly wide, hanging close to the cheeks with no tendency to stand up or out. The ear leather is thin and approximately long enough to reach the tip of the nose. Correct ear set is on a level with the eye and not too far back on the skull. The **skull** is medium-length and fairly broad, flat on top and slightly rounded at the sides and back.

On the boat.

The occiput bone is inconspicuous. As the skull rises from the foreface, it makes a stop, divided by a groove, or fluting between the eyes. The groove disappears as it reaches the middle of the forehead. The amount of stop is moderate. It must not be a pronounced feature; rather it is a subtle rise where the muzzle joins the upper head. It is emphasized by the groove and by the position and shape of the eyebrows, which are well-developed. The muzzle is approximately the same length as the skull and one half the width of the skull. Viewed in profile, the topline of the skull and muzzle lie in approximately parallel planes. The nasal bone is straight, with no inclination downward toward the tip of the nose, the latter giving an undesirable "downfaced" look. Neither is the nasal bone concave, resulting in a "dish-faced" profile; nor convex, giving the dog a Roman nose. The cheeks are flat, and the face is well-chiseled under the eye. **Jaws** are of sufficient length to allow the dog to carry game easily: fairly square, lean and strong. The upper lips come down full and rather square to cover the line of the lower jaw; however, the lips are never pendulous or exaggerated. The **nose** is fully pigmented, liver or black in color, depending on the color of the coat. The nostrils are well-opened and broad. **Teeth** are strong, clean, of good size and ideally meet in a close scissors bite. An even bite or one or two incisors slightly out of line are minor faults. Undershot, overshot and wry jaws are serious faults and are to be severely penalized.

Neck, Topline, Body: The **neck** is moderately long, muscular, clean and slightly arched at the crest. It blends gradually and smoothly into sloping shoulders. The portion of the topline from withers to tail is firm and slopes very gently. The body is short-coupled, strong and compact. The **chest** is deep, reaching the level of the elbows, with well-developed forechest; however, it is not so wide or round as to interfere with the action of the front legs. Ribs are fairly long, springing gradually to the middle of the body, then tapering as they approach the end of the ribbed section. The underline stays level with the elbows to a slight upcurve at the flank. The **back** is straight, strong and essentially level. Loins are strong, short and slightly arched. **Hips** are nicely rounded, blending smoothly into the hind legs. The croup slopes gently to the set of the tail, and tail-set

In the snow.

On the sofa.

follows the natural line of the croup. The **tail** is carried horizontally or slightly elevated and displays a characteristic, lively, merry, action particularly when the dog is on game. A clamped tail (indicating timidity or unpredictable temperament) is to be faulted, as is a tail carried at a right angle to the backline in Terrier fashion.

Forequarters: Efficient movement in front calls for proper forequarter assembly. The shoulder blades are flat and fairly close together at the tips, molding smoothly into the contour of the body. Ideally, when measured from the top of the withers to the point of the shoulder to elbow, the shoulder blade and upper arm are apparent equal length, forming an angle of nearly 90 degrees; this sets the front legs well under the body and places the elbows directly beneath the tips of the shoulder blades. Elbows lie close to the body. Forelegs are straight with the same degree of size continuing to the foot. Bone is strong, slightly flattened, not too round or too heavy. Pasterns are short, strong and slightly sloping, with no suggestion of weakness. Dewclaws are usually removed. Feet are round or slightly oval. They are compact and well-arched, of medium size with thick pads, and well-feathered between the toes.

Hindquarters: The Springer should be worked and shown in hard, muscular condition with well-developed hips and thighs. His whole rear assembly suggests strength and driving power. **Thighs** are broad and muscular. Stifle joints are strong. For functional efficiency, the angulation of the hindquarters is never greater than the forequarter, and not appreciably less. The hock joints are somewhat rounded, not small and sharp in contour. Rear pasterns are short (about

The Springer's sturdy bone structure encourages his erect carriage.

The well-muscled English Springer can hunt for hours without tiring.

one-third the distance from the hip joint to the foot) and strong, with good bone. When viewed from behind, the rear pasterns are parallel. Dewclaws are usually removed. The feet are the same as in front, except that they are smaller and often more compact.

Coat: The Springer has an outer coat and an undercoat. On the body, the outer coat is of medium length, flat or wavy, and is easily distinguishable from the undercoat, which is short, soft and dense. The quantity of undercoat is affected by climate and season. When in combination, outer coat and undercoat serve to make the dog substantially waterproof, weatherproof and thornproof. On ears, chest, legs and belly the Springer is nicely furnished with a fringe of feathering of moderate length and heaviness. On the head, front of the forelegs, and below the hock joints on the front of the hind legs, the hair is short and fine. The coat has the clean, glossy "live" appearance indicative of good health. It is legitimate to trim about the head, ears, neck, and feet, to remove dead undercoat, and to thin and shorten excess feathering as required to enhance a smart, functional appearance. The tail may be trimmed or well-fringed with wavy feathering. Above all, the appearance should be natural. Overtrimming, especially the body coat, or any chopped, barbered or artificial effect is to be penalized in the show ring, as is excessive feathering that destroys a clean outline desirable in a sporting dog. Correct quality and condition of coat is to take precedence over quantity of coat.

Color: All the following combinations of colors and markings are equally acceptable. Black or liver with white markings or predominately white with black or liver markings; blue or liver roan; tricolor; black and white or liver and white with tan markings, usually found on eyebrows, cheeks, inside of ears, and under the tail. Any white portion of the coat may be flecked with ticking. Off colors such as lemon, red or orange are not to place.

Gait: The final test of a Springer's conformation and soundness is proper movement.

Balance is a prerequisite to good movement. The front and rear assemblies must be equivalent in angulation and muscular development for the gait to be smooth and effortless. Shoulders that are well-laid back to permit a long stride are just as essential as the excellent rear quarters that provide driving power. Seen from the side, the Springer exhibits long ground-covering stride and carries a firm back, with no tendency to cross or interfere. From behind, the rear legs reach well under the body, following on a line with the forelegs. As speed increases, there is a natural tendency for the legs to converge toward a center line of travel. Movement faults include high-stepping, waster motion; short, choppy stride, crabbing; and moving with the feet wide, the latter giving roll or swing to the body.

Temperament: The typical Springer is friendly, eager to please, quick to learn and willing to obey. Such traits are conducive to tractability, which is essential for appropriate handler control in the field. In the show ring, he should exhibit poise and attentiveness and permit himself to be examined by the judge without resentment or cringing. Aggression towards people and aggression towards other dogs is not in keeping with a sporting dog's character and purpose and is not acceptable. Excessive timidity, with due allowance for puppies and novice exhibits, is to be equally penalized.

Summary: In evaluating the English Springer Spaniel, the overall picture is a primary consideration. One should look for type, which includes general appearance and outline, and also for soundness, which includes movement and temperament. Inasmuch as the dog with a smooth easy gait must be reasonably sound and well-balanced, he is to be highly regarded,

All around good companion.

however, not to the extent of forgiving him for not looking like an English Springer Spaniel. An atypical dog, too short or long in leg length or foreign in head or expression, may move well, but he is not to be preferred over a good all-round specimen that has a minor fault in movement. It must be remembered that the English Springer Spaniel is first and foremost a sporting dog of the Spaniel family, and he must look, behave and move in character.

Terms You Should Know

bitch: A female dog

brisket: The part of the body below the chest, between the forelegs, closest to the ribs

cow-hocks: When the hocks turn toward each other

dog: A male dog; also used collectively to designate both male and female

haw: A third eyelid or membrane in the inside corner of the eye

hock: The dog's true heel

leather: The flap of the ear

loin: Region of the body between the last ribs and the hindquarters

pastern: That part of the foreleg between the wrist and the toes

roach back: A convex curve of the back

scissors bite: The outside of the lower teeth touch the inside of the upper teeth

stifle: The dog's knee

topline: From just behind the withers to the tail set

withers: The highest point of the shoulder

Retrieving and Tracking

Most Springers love water. Few are gun shy, making them excellent hunting companions. Indeed, Springers are thought to show more versatility in their hunting abilities than other gundogs. Although primarily bred as a pheasant hunter, the Springer is equally capable when hunting rabbits, quail, partridge, and ducks.

Its keen sense of smell enables the Springer to follow old body-scent tracks as well as dirty tracks (trails recently hunted by other dogs). Even as puppies, some Springers are rarely stopped by a fence; they either climb over it or search for a way around it when on a trail.

The English Springer is a duck dog. It loves the water, loves the chase, and loves being out of doors. It has a highly developed sense of smell that can follow the footfall of game and track it to its source. Its two-layer coat enables the Springer to be comfortable on drizzly winter mornings as well as on humid summer afternoons.

Family Pet

The Springer is amiable, affectionate, and good tempered. Although bred for the outdoors, it can, with proper attention and exercise, adapt to life in an apartment or suburban home.

Guard Dog

Perhaps the Springer is not as protective of its perimeters as some breeds, but it is nevertheless a good watchdog. Both friends and strangers find their arrival announced long before they approach the front door. Ever loyal to its family, a properly trained Springer will assume the role of yard sitter to the children of the house.

Communicating with Your Springer

Dogs understand a limited number of words and phrases—experts set the number at 12 or fewer. Some owners claim that their dogs understand over 100 words and phrases. However extensive the vocabulary claimed, all agree on one thing: what is most important is

Ah! Right there, yes!

not what you say but how you say it. Words intended to be commands or instructions should be short, preferably one syllable, and decisively spoken. Commands accompanied by hand gestures and your own body language are the most effective of all.

How to Speak Dog

If you wish your dog, Brownie, to stop, for instance, telling her to *"Stay!"* while lifting a palm in imitation of a traffic patrolman's gesture for stop, is more effective than the spoken word alone.

Although television shows occasionally feature dogs that "talk," "sing," or "count," such entertaining displays require a certain indulgence on the part of the observer. What the animals have exhibited is a desire to please

their owners. Your dog "talks" to you by barking, whining, growling, or other verbalizations. The following list contains some of the most common meanings:

Growling: If soft and understated can mean, "Back off, I'm tired (sleepy, hungry)" or "I'm ready to play." If harsh and sharp, "Stop! Don't do that anymore!"

Barking: If the barking is in rapid sequence, one bark right after another, the dog might be telling you, "I've encountered an unusual situation—come and see." Of course, an unusual situation can mean anything from the presence of an intruder, to a full moon rising, to conversing with other dogs, to a desire to root out rooting armadillos.

Whimpering: Usually means, "I'm scared, I'm lonely," or "I'm hurt." A whimper that is more a

Small Children

Small children, of course, must learn how to maneuver around a large dog. Monitor the child's behavior until you are sure all is well. Teach the child to respect the dog and to recognize when the dog has had enough.

You will find that the Springer is amazingly forgiving of small mistakes. He is also wise enough to leave an uncomfortable situation. If Brownie comes to you followed by a complaining child trying to hold onto her tail, listen to her side of it. Distract the child and separate the two for awhile. Even an easygoing Springer like Brownie needs a break.

Springer meets toddler.

whine often means, "I need to go out. Stop the car (or Open the house door)."

Body Language

Your dog, Brownie, also "talks" to you and to other animals by a sequence of body signals common to all breeds. Some of these easily read communications are

Staring: If your own dog stares at you while you are trying to discipline her, she is sending a confrontational signal. Stare back and do not be the first one to look away. If an unfamiliar dog sends this signal with accompanying aggressive sounds, don't stare back. Avoid eye contact. In other words, if a dog attempts to "stare you down" and that stare is accompanied by other signs of aggression, do not accept the challenge. Leave the area.

Tail-wagging: If Brownie wags her tail she is offering a friendly greeting. Conversely, if a dog holds his body stiffly and stands with his tail stiff and straight, the dog is ready to make or accept a challenge.

Crouching: If Brownie or any other dog assumes a crouching position, almost taking a bow with her front legs forward and her head lowered, she is inviting you to play.

Lying on Back: If Brownie lies on her back at your feet, exposing her stomach, she is showing submission to your authority.

The Springer and Children

Few of us want to kennel our Springers full time. Indeed, even those owners and their pets involved in hunting, dog shows, or field trials, recognize the value of close contact between the animals and their human families. At the end of the day many wind up in the kitchen, or

Dressed to go.

in front of the television set with the family.

The Springer loves attention. He will lie down and stretch to full body length for anyone willing to scratch his belly or his sides, or tickle him under the chin. Conversely, he will be a willing companion in countless games of fetch and run. Brownie will bound out the door ahead of you, and run back as if to say, "Why are you so slow? Let's go!"

The Springer and Other Pets

There shouldn't be any problem associated with introducing a Springer to other household pets. Springers have been known to share their quarters with cats, puppies, and other breeds.

It will be easier for you to bring a new puppy into the house than a full grown dog. Wise owners introduce a new pet slowly and affectionately. You will find that female dogs are often more territorial than the males, frequently resisting and often terrorizing a newcomer.

If you live or visit in the country, you would probably not want to give your Springers the run of a yard inhabited by turkeys, chickens, or other feathered fowl. In the same vein, a farm pond filled with chattering, preening waterfowl is just a big playpen for a Springer. You wouldn't want to bring a Springer into a household in which normally caged birds are occasionally allowed loose, either. Just remember the dog's heritage—Brownie's own instinct and countless generations of training and

selective breeding have embedded in her a desire to catch and silence that fluttering wing.

Summary

A Springer lover, summing up a heated discussion with two friends dedicated to Irish Setters and Labrador Retrievers, said, "What you have to understand is, my Springer doesn't stop to point at the bird; he takes off running and grabs hold of it. And he can keep up with any Lab in the water and swim circles around some of them. At home, he loves my kids, and he barks when friend or foe comes up to the gate. What more do you want of a dog? Maybe other dogs can do one or two things better, but for an all-around companion, I wouldn't trade my English Springer Spaniel for any other breed."

YOUR NEW PUPPY

Springer puppies are charming, fun-loving animals bent on exploring every inch of land, tasting every fallen leaf, and turning over every stick in reach.

The decision to adopt a puppy is not made without thoughtful consideration.

✔ Puppies disrupt our daily routines—we can no longer just get up and go.

✔ Puppies take a lot of our time. Somebody has to feed a puppy and to clean up after it.

✔ Puppies chew on things, litter the yard, scratch doors.

✔ Training a puppy involves somebody doing some research and then having some time to put that research into effect.

✔ Puppies are expensive. After the initial purchase, food, veterinarians, and fencing add an additional cost.

Why would anyone ever go to the trouble of house-training a noisy, litterbug of a puppy? Obviously for some people, the negative aspects of dog ownership are far outweighed by the positive ones. Puppies are loving, adventuresome, tireless creatures. Puppies are responsive, inquisitive beings capable of experiencing and offering happiness, pride, and satisfaction.

Playtime.

Puppies mature into loyal canine companions that sit at our side as we work our own way through life, seeming to share our joys and sorrows.

That's why we put up with puppies—to enjoy the friendship of an animal that thinks we're great.

And the feeling is mutual. One study estimated that at least one million dogs have been named beneficiaries in wills. In reflection, writer Christopher Morley wrote, "No one appreciates the very special genius of your conversation as a dog does."

The Purchase Decision

It seems that one merely has to voice a wish for a dog and somebody knows somebody who has a new litter. "They're pretty little puppies," they'll say. "No problem."

All puppies are "pretty little puppies." How can one be sure, once the decision has been made, that you and that puppy will like each other once the newness has worn off?

Shoes are us.

Purebred or Mixed Breed?

There is nothing wrong with getting a mixed-breed dog. Mixed breeds (nicknamed "Heinz 57" in reference to a famous ketchup company) can be loving, even-tempered pets. Mixed-breed dogs have been part of our life from the beginning. After all, historically, new breeds are those "mixed" from established ones. Perhaps you can find stable, well-cared-for, mixed-breed puppies in your neighbor's backyard. The local shelter usually identifies, as closely as possible, mixed breeds up for adoption. Read your local newspaper. Chances are, you'll find a classified ad offering puppies from stray matches "free to a good home."

SPRINGER SOUNDBITES

"It is easier to preserve a canine saint than it is to reform a canine sinner."
John Kent, trainer

The problem with owning a mixed-breed dog is that we often know little about the puppy's parents, his health care, his potential abilities, or his socialization. Even so, these dogs are often intelligent, healthy, and make wonderful pets. If you do decide to adopt a mixed-breed dog, examine the dog closely. Try to identify his most dominant hereditary traits. Inquire about his parents. Ask a veterinarian to help you. Then read a book about the breed that seems closest to your pet. Much of the information on inheritable traits and the training suggestions will be valuable.

The principal benefit to owning a purebred dog is that one can predict the dog's future physical, social, and temperamental traits with some accuracy. When we hear that a purebred dog is "registered," with one of the major kennel clubs, for instance, we know that for a number of generations that dog's ancestors have been of the identical breed. We can learn a lot more than breed lineage from a dog's registration papers, and we will cover that later (see page 47). For the moment, we can presume that a registered dog, for which we have the papers, is of a certain "pure" breed. (If a dog is said to be purebred but he does not have papers, he may or may not be purebred. Without papers there is no proof that the line is unbroken.)

The American Kennel Club recognizes 150 dog breeds, divided into seven groups categorized by type. This allows a wide range of choices to prospective dog owners. For example, if you want a small lapdog you might want to consider a pet from among the 17 breeds of Group 5, toys. (Eight of the spaniels are toys; the remainder are classified as Group 1, sporting dogs.)

In summary, choosing a purebred dog gives the owner a better chance of owning a pet that matches his or her own standards and preferences.

Pet Dog, Show Dog, or Field Dog?

The only difference a professional makes between "pet" and "show" is that puppies labeled "pets" do not conform to some part of the rigid Springer standard. There are any number of reasons the dog will not make it to the show ring: the tail may not be set right, the ears may be too short, coloring and markings may be off.

Field-bred Springers must flush and retrieve pheasant, grouse, quail, partridge, and duck. The tail is shorter and the coat is clipped. The Springer works within gun range, sending birds into the air. When the new puppy is unhappy with the noise and confusion in the field or when he is plainly miserable he is withdrawn and sold as a pet dog.

Nevertheless you can trust that these pedigreed pets come from a sturdy bloodline and have the ability to earn top-notch honors in obedience, agility, fly-ball, tracking, search and rescue, or as therapy dogs. Furthermore, it is extremely unlikely that these top-pedigreed Springers will have health, energy, emotional, or personality problems. Isn't this what you want for a companion?

Kennels and Private Breeders

Some major kennels advertise on the Internet, or nationally in the classified section of magazines. Selecting a dog from a popular kennel often involves a delay of several months, perhaps because there is a waiting list, or because the right mating cannot be scheduled until a later time. Particularly if one plans to show or to

Hey, where am I?

field-train a dog, a puppy from a line of proven champions can be an excellent investment.

Private breeders usually advertise locally or within a limited area. These so-called "backyard breeders" seem to be of two kinds.

1. Family Number 1 has an even-tempered family dog, a registered female. This female is mated to a registered male, usually a local stud. Little thought is given to bloodlines, heredity, or faults. When the puppies arrive, they will be adorable. They will be thoroughly and lovingly tended to, and at seven weeks or so, sold as a result of classified advertising. This family may or may not raise another litter. Their puppies typically will not be outstanding in any way except as good family dogs.

2. Family 2 has a family dog that they show in conformation. The family is aware of breed problems and has had their female tested for hip dysplasia, eye entropion, canine brucellosis, and parasites. Through their breed clubs and show contacts the family searches for the right stud exhibiting the particular physical and temperamental characteristics that they desire.

Nap, nap, nap.

Family 2 may require prospective purchasers to have a fenced-in area, among other considerations, often rejecting buyers who don't conform to their standards. The family cares about the welfare of their puppies for life, offering health guarantees. Most will take back one of their puppies if a problem develops or the new owners can no longer care for it. Their puppies typically will be good family dogs. Some may have championship qualities.

Puppy Mills

"Puppy mills," those kennels operated by breeders who mass-produce popular breeds, often sell undersocialized puppies weaned too early. Some of these mass-production operations breed their females every season and at the very least keep poor records. In the event that one of these kennel lines develops a genetic or basic health problem, the breeders are too far away from the point of sale to be aware of it. Such puppies often can be identified by a certain listlessness and lack of the sparkle usually associated with a quality puppy. Avoid those that appear stressed or unusually highstrung.

Shelters and Rescued Dogs

Unfortunately, all too many puppies grow up in busy families who have no time to properly train their little newcomer. These puppies reach adolescence having learned only that loneliness can be cured by wailing, that teething aches can be eased by chewing whatever is handy, and, worst of all, that people can be intimidated by snarling and snapping. These puppies grow up to become misfits through no fault of their own. Their families, according to inclination, take the throw-away dog for a car ride, dropping him off at the nearest crossroads, or head for the nearest animal shelter.

When young and obviously untrained dogs are dropped off at the shelter, those dedicated workers assess the dog.

✔ Is he healthy?
✔ Has he been mistreated?
✔ Is he purebred?
✔ Is he aggressive?
✔ Would the dog, if trained, make a good family pet?

The staff will work with local breed clubs to place the dog with another family. In their effort to reduce the number of free-roaming pets, many shelters require that the dog be spayed or neutered before placing it for adoption. If the dog is too young for the procedure, payment is taken in advance and a temporary certificate is issued. Dogs that can't be placed fall into the statistical six million dogs a year destroyed in shelters.

Age, Sex, Temperament

Few can resist the appeal of a puppy. The charm of a young animal overpowers the resistance of the most reluctant. The responsibility of feeding, training, and caring for a youngster is often the last consideration for the smitten. Those who do have the time and inclination to raise a puppy are rewarded by the sure pleasure of watching a young animal grow and develop into a well-trained, handsome adult.

Let us not forget, however, the older dog that often, through no fault of his own, loses his home and goes back on the market. People move, retire, travel, lose their jobs, enter nursing homes, all reasons for not being able to care for a dog. They search among their family and acquaintances for someone to take over the dog's care. When all else fails, these families take their pets, ideal candidates for adoption, to the local shelter.

Occasionally, aggressive adolescent dogs, from 9 to 13 months of age, that have not received the proper training, are brought to shelters. Strong, confident owners, with the assistance of a professional trainer, can redeem these wayward juveniles, transforming them into the canine good citizens they are capable of becoming.

The question is often asked: Are male or female dogs better as pets? The answer is complicated. Both sexes can be equally well trained and equally affectionate. Female Springers usually come into heat twice a year and must be confined. Males often roam the neighborhood and beyond in instinctive response to that distracting lure of a female in heat. Both of these potential problems can be handled by the owner. The female can be spayed, and the male can be neutered, and they often will be better pets for it.

As far as temperament goes, either sex can be aggressive, either can be possessive, either can be boisterous, either can be lazy. Behavior

depends partly on heredity, partly on environment and training. With the exception of genetic abnormalities, the eventual temperament of the dog is pretty much up to you.

Puppy Aptitude Testing

Every day, students of animal behavior learn a little more about the dog. Moreover, studies of young animals have helped psychologists in their work with children. Behaviorists around the world share information on procedures and techniques designed to help us understand the world's oldest domesticated animal. In 1963 Clarence Pfaffenberger, in an effort to develop guidelines for his work at Guide Dogs for the Blind, published the results of his studies on dog behavior. When the institute began its work with dogs, only 8 percent of the dogs enrolled in the program graduated successfully. Consequently, Pfaffenberger set out first to

Home, sweet home.

Family portrait.

define the personality traits possessed by successful Guide Dogs, and then to identify those tendencies in puppies. Within a few years, with work, study, and clinical assistance, new statistics emerged. Today, more than 90 percent of the puppies selected complete the Guide Dog training. What caused this amazing turnaround, and how can we learn from it?

Dog behavior testing is based on close observation of the puppy at certain ages of his development, and under standardized conditions. Behaviorists have proven for instance, that there are certain times in his life when a dog can do his best learning. Puppies, for instance, cannot be taught much before they are 21 days old. From 21 to 49 days (three to seven weeks), however, a puppy will do his best learning, either with your help, or by himself. The secret is, to be present during those periods when the puppy can best accept guidance.

Is This the Puppy for You?

When choosing your puppy, remember that a Springer is a sporting dog. Daily, focused activity will improve his spirits, his disposition, and his muscle tone. He will enjoy vigorous play sessions and long walks. He will respond enthusiastically to training challenges.

The puppy's confidence, or social attraction, is measured by how readily and happily a strange puppy will come to you.

1. Place the puppy in the center of an area and step away from him.

2. Kneel down and gently clap your hands. How quickly the puppy comes, or whether he comes at all, are both reflections of his social independence.

3. Next, see if the puppy will follow you. Walk away from him in a normal manner and do not call to him. Be sure he sees you walk away. Failure to follow, or lack of interest, reveals the puppy's degree of following attraction.

Will the puppy accept restraint? Turn the puppy over, belly up. With one hand, hold the puppy down for 30 seconds. Does he lie submissively? Does he struggle for awhile and then lie submissively? How hard does he struggle?

Do you want a more dominant or a more submissive pet?

Stroking: Can you stroke the puppy from head to tail without him jumping up, growling, or nipping at you? Does he just walk away from you? Does he accept this stroking, which is a sign of social dominance on your part?

With both hands pick up the puppy and hold him just off the ground for at least 30 seconds. You are now in total control. How well does the puppy accept elevation dominance? Does he wiggle, nip, or wait patiently?

An extremely dominant dog, one that scores high in all categories, is a poor choice for families with small children, or for elderly people. If properly trained and if he is part of a calm, adult household, these dogs make wonderful pets.

Conversely, a dog that shows a high degree of submission must also be in the proper household. Although these dogs have few aggressive tendencies, their low level of confidence will require plenty of praise during training, and thoughtful handling to bring out their latent confidence.

These preceding tests indicate the importance of observing a dog carefully before you bring him home. Each breed has tendencies, but each dog is an individual. These guidelines, and your breeder's help, can provide a basis for your decision. Most breeders today use a combination of some kind of testing and personal, up-close evaluation and can be of tremendous help to you when making your selection.

Bringing Your Pet Home

Before the big day arrives, a thoughtful owner will have on hand a few basic puppy necessities such as food and a bowl to put it in, a water dish, and a comfortable bed. Later the puppy will need a brush, a collar and leash, and perhaps a toy or two.

Bring your puppy home when someone, preferably the primary caregiver, has two or three days to spend with him. The puppy will be lonesome for his littermates. He will miss the warmth and sleeping companionship of a box full of puppies. It is up to you, his new owner, to make him feel welcome and at home.

A Place of His Own

As a new member of your family, your puppy will appreciate knowing the rules. It is best to make some thoughtful decisions even before the puppy arrives, and it is very important to be consistent when applying these rules. Basic considerations regarding where the puppy will sleep, where he will eliminate, who will feed him, and who will train him must be addressed ahead of time.

When you arrive home, take the puppy right away to the place you have selected for him to eliminate in. Wait while he does his business, which shouldn't be long coming. Praise the puppy, play with him, scoop him up in your arms, and take him into the house.

The Bed

The puppy's bed should be located in a quiet corner away from the house traffic patterns but near the family's activity center. He will want to be a part of any function to the point that he will risk getting stepped on to participate.

Unless you intend to crate-train your puppy, it is not necessary to purchase a special bed for the puppy's use. Wicker baskets are pretty, but a young spaniel can be quite destructive. It is better to begin with a soft nest of towels and a cardboard box for awhile. Later you can upgrade when necessary. Cut out a small door in the box, turn it upside down, and allow the puppy to crawl inside. Your puppy will feel safe in this makeshift cave and spend many hours in it. If you do intend to crate-train your puppy, and we suggest that the long-term benefits are of great value to both of you, suggestions follow.

The Crate as Hearth and Home

The purpose of a crate is to simulate a den. Don't be misled by the comparison of a crated puppy to a caged zoo animal deprived of any freedom. Pay no attention to those who commiserate with the puppy on his confinement. Enjoy instead the knowledge that you have selected a proven aid to puppy rearing. Used properly, crating works for both worlds. You will soon realize that your puppy enjoys his crate, indeed will return to it voluntarily, seeing in it a secure haven, a place he can hide in when overwhelmed by stomping, threatening feet. A crate is a quiet place where a puppy can nap without worry, knowing his family is nearby. You yourself will learn to appreciate the crate as a house-training tool of enormous importance.

Crate Training

Those owners who elect to crate-train their puppies will receive quicker response and will

be more pleased with learning retention than those using other methods. The concept behind crate training is to replace the den image embedded in the animal's brain. A den represents to an animal the security from predators and comfort from the elements that he instinctively seeks. For lucky pets and their owners, crates are not just a method of house-training, but a way of life.

Sizes and materials: Crates, available from pet supply stores and from catalogs, are made in many sizes and of several materials. Collapsible metal or fiberglass crates tend to be the most popular. For economy's sake select a crate that will accommodate a full grown Springer, at least 3 feet (.9 m) long. (A larger size will not bother the puppy.) Because you can expect your Springer to stand approximately 26 to 27 inches (65–67 cm) tall, his crate should be no less than 30 inches (75 cm) high.

Location: Have the crate on hand before you bring the puppy home.

✔ Don't try to set up a crate for the very young puppy in the garage or in a room shut off from the family. He will be profoundly unhappy.

✔ Set it up in a location from which the puppy can see the family activity, yet one that will be out of the main traffic flow. A corner of the kitchen or family room is fine.

✔ Inside the crate, place a washable mat or rug for the puppy to lie down on. If you like, you may include a chew toy, but this is not necessary at the outset. Do not put any food or water in the crate.

How long? Lengthen crate time gradually. Even at 16 weeks of age, two hours is the maximum crate time for a puppy unless he is deeply asleep. Keep an ear open for sounds. Although puppies do sleep a lot, they periodically awaken to eliminate and search for food, water, and attention.

Cleaning Up After Your Pet

Accidents will happen. If you see the puppy dribbling, pick him up immediately, saying *"No!"* in a very firm voice and carry him, still dribbling if necessary, to his elimination spot. Because puppies are creatures of habit, and because they return to the "scene of the crime," douse the spot with an odor eliminator. Several chemical solutions are on the market and all work well if applied immediately. The combination of bacteria and enzyme in some removes the odor and actually "eats" the organic matter.

If you do not have access to or do not wish to use one of the enzyme products, we can suggest several homemade remedies. Two that are proven to work are ordinary powdered cornstarch or a solution of diluted vinegar. Whatever product you select, the procedures described next are essentially the same for all.

Cornstarch
✔ If the accident is on a carpet, blot as much moisture as you can with an old towel or several layers of paper toweling.
✔ Press down with your foot in order remove as much moisture as possible from the padding. If you are using an enzyme, follow the manufacturer's directions.
✔ If you decide to use cornstarch, dry the spot as much as possible and then layer on a generous amount.
✔ Cover the spot and let dry. Vacuum later. The cornstarch will have absorbed the moisture and the odor.

Not by the Ears
One U.S. president received a lot of attention from the press when he was photographed lifting his pet beagles by the ears. Although the beagles didn't howl, animal lovers did. You wouldn't pick your Springer up by those marvelous ears, but we can hurt our puppies in other ways by not following the correct lifting procedures.

Puppies are wiggly, unwieldy fur balls. Some puppies resent being lifted off the floor. Some are frightened. When the puppies squirm trying to free themselves, they may be dropped.

The proper way to lift a puppy is to use two hands. Place one hand under the puppy's heavy little bottom and place the other hand on the puppy's chest between the front legs. The puppy is almost in a sitting position. Don't let anyone grab the puppy around the stomach to lift him; don't let anyone lift the puppy by the scruff of the neck and please, not by the ears!

Teach children not to lift the puppy by his front legs, his stomach, and certainly not by his ears.

Smile for the camera.

Vinegar

✔ The vinegar treatment requires that the rug be colorfast. Test it on an inconspicuous corner first to be sure.

✔ Mix one part of vinegar to two parts of water. Pour onto the spot approximately as much vinegar as there was urine.

✔ Allow the solution to sit for five minutes.

✔ Again, blot all the moisture with a towel or paper toweling.

✔ Weigh down and let dry. The odor should be gone.

Note: First, never use a product containing ammonia to clean up a urine odor. It is the ammonia in the urine that we are trying to remove. Second, perform the cleanup activity after the puppy is out of the room. And third, keep the puppy away from the spot at least overnight.

The Right Toys

Puppies are playful animals, chasing leaves, squirrels, and birds with equal joy. We enjoy watching our puppies at play and often join them at their games, providing them with balls and specially made chew toys. Puppies with freedom to run in the yard don't need many special toys, however, as long as they have an assortment of sticks, leaves, and pinecones to play with. A puppy soon selects a favorite stick, for instance, carries it around for hours, sets it down, and loses it. Some time later, even days later, the stick will reappear; the puppy will carry it proudly, gnaw it for awhile, and again abandon it for a squirrel chase.

We should be cautious about giving a puppy lightweight plastic toys that shred easily. Puppies have been known to tear off and swallow whistles, noisemakers, and button eyes from furry toys. Some authorities recommend offering the puppy an old leather glove to chew on. It has your smell and you probably misplaced the mate, anyway. Do try to avoid giving your puppy an old shoe, however. While you are unlikely to leave your new gloves lying around, your shoes are often on the floor. Your puppy cannot distinguish between a shoe you will permit him to chew on and a new pair of shoes.

We provided our family's puppies with chew hooves, which were instant favorites, an assortment of hard vinyl bones that we removed before they splintered, and homemade toys such as knotted white cotton socks. One favorite trick is to tie a sock around a canning jar ring. The combination has a satisfactory carry-handle and makes a wonderful clanking noise when dragged on the floor.

Learning to Stay Alone

Your puppy is a social animal. He grew up in a litter and will not want to stay alone. Bereft of his mother and littermates, he will set up a lonesome wail for company. Although this part of puppy training is sometimes the hardest, and a few sleepless hours are to be expected, those who have been there before us have left a few helpful suggestions to help us make it through.

The First Nights

He is your puppy. He will be your 40- or 50-pound (18–23 kg) dog. If you don't mind your Springer sleeping in the bedroom with you, bring him in, by all means. If you do want to train him to sleep alone, be very matter of fact about your wishes.

✔ Be sure the puppy eliminates late in the evening, preferably right before your bedtime.
✔ Take him to his bed, cuddle him, give him a chance to settle down, then go out and close the door. Don't go far. Chances are the puppy will demand that you return.
✔ Go back in. Talk to the puppy. Reassure him, cuddle him, and leave again.

TIP

Helpful Hints

Because puppy lovers understand that the puppy longs for companionship, noise, closeness, and warmth, owners have been very inventive in trying to replace in his life whatever will reproduce these conditions. You might find some of the following suggestions helpful.
✔ Place a ticking clock nearby.
✔ Tune a radio to an all-night talk station.
✔ Donate an old, unwashed sweatshirt to the nest.
✔ Wrap a hot water bottle in a soft towel.
✔ Provide a favorite chew toy.
✔ Close your bedroom door.

✔ Here's the hard part: If the puppy continues to wail, the last thing you want to do is to give it the impression that you will return on call. This time, if you are sure he is fed and doesn't have to eliminate, knock sharply on the door and call out *"No!"* The point is to startle the puppy into seeing a relationship between his fussing and the loud noise. He also gets the idea that his new friend is displeased. The puppy may be so weary that he will curl up and go to sleep until early, very early, the next morning. Consider yourself lucky.

Dogs are naturally clean animals. That statement may sound funny at first, especially if you have ever had to clean up a floor or a carpet after a pet has had an "accident" on it. Observe the mother of a litter as she demonstrates the truth of that belief, however.

The Mother of the Litter

When the puppies are born, the mother cleans them up and eats the afterbirth. She frequently licks, massages, and turns her puppies, thus forcing them to move, breathe, and eliminate. So powerful is the force driving her that for two weeks she rarely leaves the puppies, but perseveres with licking and massaging them, forcing them to eliminate and disposing of the waste.

At about three weeks of age, however, the puppies are somewhat ambulatory. The mother's natural instinct for cleanliness, enforced by a sharp nip if necessary, convinces the puppies to eliminate some distance away from the central gathering place. The accepted distance gets progressively farther until even the laziest puppy is motivated to eliminate outside the nest.

Animal behaviorists tell us that we can take advantage of this learned puppy behavior of not soiling his own bed by adapting this early training to the puppy's new environment.

Suggestions

The following are suggestions that have worked for others. It is very hard to generalize because your Springer

puppy is not like any other Springer puppy. Your puppy may handle stress differently than other puppies do. Moreover, you may be very experienced and need no assistance in raising puppies. But for the first-time puppy owner, the suggestions that follow will help. By understanding what is happening between you and the puppy, these suggestions can be modified and personalized to fit your needs.

Be consistent: Feed the puppy at the same times every day. Take him to the same place outside every time he needs to eliminate. Take the puppy in and out the same door. And stay with him. If you put the puppy out and go back inside, he will likely wait on the steps until you let him back in and then finish his business in the house.

Be enthusiastic: Praise the puppy. Cuddle him. Talk to him. Laugh with him. Play with him. Make that puppy want to please you more than anything else in life. Be sure he knows when you are pleased. Stroke him. Nuzzle him. Be a friend.

Be observant: Take advantage of the puppy's natural instincts. Watch for signs of discomfort. Even a very young

With patience, both puppy and family will agree on the proper elimination process.

puppy (six or seven weeks old) when confined to a crate, will bark and whine when he has to eliminate. He will do his best to avoid soiling his bed.

In daytime he must eliminate after every nap, every meal, and every play session. It may seem like you're on call every two or three hours all day. Nevertheless, train yourself in the daytime to respond to the early signals. Watch for sniffing along the floor or walking in circles, both obvious signs that the search is on.

Be cool: Your puppy will do everything within his limited understanding to please you. But when, not if, you come home to an "accident," your puppy will take one look at you, tuck his tail, and try to hide behind the sofa. You might think "he knows what he did wrong." No, actually, he does not know. He is hiding because he is scared of you. As calmly as you can, remove the puppy from the scene and clean up the mess by yourself. Do not, no matter how aggravated you are, threaten him with the mess, fuss at, shake, or otherwise discipline the puppy. For sure, don't rub his nose in it. Be patient and try again. One day it will all work out.

Be smart: Don't let the puppy get overstimulated. As soon as everyone has greeted and petted the puppy, reclaim him. Put the puppy in his crate for about ten minutes. Speak softly to him, and go about your business, keeping within his hearing range. The puppy should fall asleep. If, despite your best efforts, the puppy is still awake and is whimpering, take him out, cuddle him, talk to him, and then put him back in the crate for another ten minutes or so.

Paper Training

Teaching your puppy to eliminate outdoors is the best way to reduce messy accidents in the house. Some family situations, however, such as

A puppy will learn not to soil his bed.

bad weather, apartment living, or work routines, lend themselves more conveniently to paper training.

The basic theory behind paper training is to teach the puppy to eliminate on the newspaper and *only* on the newspaper. Because puppies instinctively seek out a spot that has been used before, your task is to select that spot before the puppy does, and to remind the puppy of its location.

Your puppy will have poor marksmanship in the beginning; therefore you must cover a fairly wide area with paper. A thick layer, double-page size is usually sufficient.

The procedure is the same as for outside. Take the puppy to his spot and wait with him until the deed has been performed. Praise the puppy when he has completed the job. Take the puppy out of the room. Then, later, remove the soiled sheets, leaving behind the bottom sheets that will still retain the odors. Place these bottom sheets on top of the next stack of papers, and so on.

THE ADULT SPRINGER

Even the cutest Springer puppy is destined to be a loopy, gangly adolescent before he is a mature, responsible companion. How does he make the transition? How can you help?

General Care

Unless groomed for a show career, Willie, the family Springer that spends most of his time indoors, does not need intensive shaping or trimming. His coat will thin in response to the indoor climate. Springers kept in outdoor kennels all winter, including those that frequently hunt, however, do grow a full, wooly coat and will benefit from some trimming around the toe pads, topknot, and tail each spring.

Provided Willie stays away from mud puddles, skunks, and garbage cans he will rarely require a bath. Generally speaking, a twice-weekly brushing with a medium bristle brush should remove matted hair and keep his waterproof coat in good shape. Besides, your dog will love the attention. Willie's pendulous ears, on the other hand, do demand rather more frequent attention than some breeds.

Barring any unusual circumstances, the following schedule should keep your dog clean, healthy, and pest free.

Ready for the hunt.

Clipping

There are two kinds of clipping patterns, pet and field trim and show trim. For pets, electric clippers are used on the head, neck, and back. Because clipping coarsens the coat, most groomers recommend that if you start with clippers, plan to continue with clippers. On show dogs, clippers are used only on the head, throat, and tops of ears. The outer coat is allowed to grow long. The undercoat is stripped with knives or thinning scissors to remove dead hair. Feathering on the legs and tail add to the Springer's attractiveness.

An occasional clipping of ear hair and hair between the toes will help your Springer feel better. Occasional attention to the topknot and the tip of the tail will help your pet look better, too.

It is important to start early. A very young Springer can learn to stand quietly for his trim and to enjoy the massage and attention that follows. Alternatively, dogs not introduced at a young age to the noise of clippers and blow dryers will have a difficult time adjusting to even basic grooming procedures.

Grooming

At least twice a week brush your puppy from head to tail with a medium bristle brush. Springers have a double coat and the outer hair is fairly long. Frequent brushing removes sticks, burrs, and stray weed seeds that attach themselves to ears, tails, and underbellies. The unbrushed, untrimmed Springer soon develops a mat of dead hair that is unsightly, uncomfortable, and difficult to untangle. Pay particular attention to the armpit mats.

Books are available detailing the Springer cuts, but the personal advice of a professional

SPRINGER SOUNDBITES

"It must be remembered that there never has been a 'perfect' dog, but it is possible to greatly improve any dog with proper trimming."
Julia Gasow, breeder

Off to the groomer.

is not to be ignored. These groomers provide the experience and attention to detail that many Springer owners desire for their pets. Their advice can be indispensable. Dedicated owners with advice, experience, and patience can learn to keep their Springers in good trim, but an occasional trip to the beauty parlor helps everyone.

Bathing

When the inevitable time comes that Willie will need a bath, you will know it.

When you wash your Springer, prepare to do a thorough job, taking care of all the odds and ends that somehow get lost these busy days. Old clothes, old towels, a mild commercial dog shampoo, lukewarm water, and plenty of elbow room are prime requisites. Have on hand some cotton to stuff in his ears, some swabs to clean out his ears and eyes, a nail clipper for toenails, and a medium bristle brush.

✔ First, brush the dog thoroughly.

✔ Examine him for fleas, ticks, and hot spots (patches of bare skin that weep and cause pain).

✔ Look for bruises or unusual lumps or tender places.

✔ Check your dog's feet. Trim any unnecessary hair from around his toes. Trim his toenails if necessary.

✔ Begin the actual bath by lathering a ring around the dog's neck. This will prevent any fleas or other critters that are scurrying to escape from the soap from gathering on the dog's face.

✔ Move on to the back and stomach. Don't forget to pay special attention to the tail, the toes, and armpits.

✔ The secret to a good wash is a good rinse. Don't leave a soap residue on the dog. Rinse and rinse again.

✔ If the day is warm, let Willie run for awhile and shake off the excess water before towel-drying him. In bad weather, towel-dry him immediately, and keep him inside at least overnight.

Ears

Inspect Willie's long and lovely ears every day. Keep the hair short underneath the earflap to allow air circulation. If he drags his ears through his food bowl, consider a narrower dish or tie back his earflaps closer to his head with a bandanna.

Inspect the interior of his ears at least every week. Clean inside the ear with a cotton ball or a Q-tip dipped in a proprietary mixture or in a homemade solution of 1/2 alcohol and 1/2 white vinegar. If you use a Q-tip, don't stick the end in the ear any farther than you can see. Pay attention to the color of the earwax. Brown earwax is probably normal. Black wax, resembling coffee grounds, could mean ear mites. Yellow or green may indicate an infection.

Eyes

Pay special attention to your Springer's eyes. Even after a day of traveling through land no more foreign than the brush of your backyard, the weed seeds and biting insects can make a dog's life miserable. If you suspect a problem, call your veterinarian.

Teeth and Nails

Teeth: Don't forget to brush Willie's teeth. Although dogs don't get cavities, a gum disease called gingivitis, caused by a buildup of

Bath time.

Brush those mats and tangles.

Ready to go again.

Then add a bit of toothpaste. Allow him to lick the toothpaste off the brush. Then reapply the paste and begin brushing with a circular motion. No flossing required!

Your pet's teeth should be professionally cleaned every two to three years. This will involve general anesthesia so it is to your benefit to do as much as you can to practice good dental hygiene between visits.

Nails: Toenails are an important part of good health, so keep Willie's nails short. Long nails are uncomfortable for your pet and are more likely to get caught in a fence or between the boards of the back porch.

Perhaps your pet's nails do not need a trim. This is likely if he spends a lot of time out-of-doors or on hard surfaces. The most likely indication that nails need trimming is sound: As one breeder phrased it, "If you hear a click, cut."

calculus, will eventually cause trouble. Begin brushing while Willie is still a puppy and continue to brush at least twice a week.

Purchase a doggie dental kit with a soft, nylon bristle brush. Some owners prefer special brushes that fit on a fingertip; some use a human toothbrush. Some, not many, can accustom their pets to electric brushes. Do use chicken- or beef-flavored toothpaste. Some human toothpastes contain detergents or fluoride that could be harmful. A three percent hydrogen peroxide solution, though not as tasty, will also do the job.

Don't frighten your pet. Give plenty of love and stroking while brushing. If necessary, let him carry the toothbrush around for a while.

Exercising Your Springer

If your Springer is a hunter, or a country dog blessed with endless property on which to roam, you may not need to add additional exercise to his daily routine. But if, like many of today's Springers, yours is almost housebound, or at least confined to a small backyard, your pet's health and outlook on life will benefit by an exercise program.

Walking, running, chasing, running beside your bicycle, Frisbee, and ball playing are viable forms of exercise that are both companionable and beneficial to your pet. The only warning would be a suggestion to monitor the level of effort expended. Puppies and adolescent dogs can be damaged by overexertion. Your adult

Springer can probably keep up with you. If you are exercising a puppy, however, stop at once if you see heavy panting or decreased speed.

An Outdoor Run

If Willie is an outdoor pet, you probably already have a doghouse set up near your house, so constructed and situated as to shelter him from winter winds and driving spring rains.

If you haven't constructed the kennel house yet, keep a few points in mind:

✔ Raise the floor several inches off the ground for additional air circulation in summer. Check for drafts in winter.

✔ Provide plenty of dry bedding. A chintz dog pillow looks pretty, but if the filling gets wet, your dog will get chilled. If you don't want to invest in a waterproof pillow, then clean straw, wood chips, or even shredded paper—changed once a week—make fine beds.

✔ Willie will lie facing the entrance you use most frequently, so make it easy for him. Position the kennel opening so that he faces the door or the gate you use most frequently.

✔ If you cannot fence in your entire yard, construct a dog run around the kennel. Runs can be purchased from supply houses or constructed on site of galvanized, 11-gauge, zinc-coated wire. Installing the fence on top of a narrow concrete slab will prevent your pet from digging under the fence. For Springers, an 8-by-16-foot (2.4 × 5 m) enclosed exercise run is adequate.

✔ Set the kennel house up against the garage or another solid structure for added protection from winter winds and rains.

Note: Willie is an outside dog, but on truly bitter winter nights, if his kennel has no heat, house your pet inside.

Registering Your Springer

Springers traditionally are registered through one of two national organizations, the American Kennel Club or the United Kennel Club. Write them for more information about either organization; their addresses are listed in the Information section (see page 92) of this book.

The American Kennel Club

The American Kennel Club (AKC), established in 1884, maintains a registry listing the ancestral record of each dog on its lists. This record is known as the Stud Book. When a litter is produced as the result of a mating between two registered dogs, the owner of the mother dog (the dam) notifies the AKC by completing and submitting a litter application. This application is ordinarily mailed off within a few weeks of birth, certainly no later than six weeks afterward. The AKC responds by return-

TIP

Why Bother with Registration at All?

The somewhat cumbersome routine of registration has one primary purpose: to certify purebred dogs. Each purebred Springer puppy has his own unique identification number that will follow him through life. That registration shows that all the puppy's ancestors were Springers. It shows which ancestors received which titles and certifies that they possessed certain championship qualities they may have passed on to their offspring.

All that hard work paid off.

ing to the owner a "litter" kit that includes registration applications for each puppy. This application, known as the blue form, is then turned over to the new owners. It is this blue form that the final owner sends back to the AKC (along with the appropriate fee), to request an AKC Registration Certificate, known as "papers."

The United Kennel Club

The United Kennel Club (UKC), founded in 1898, is primarily a working dog registry. The UKC also maintains a registration service, and encourages a "total dog" philosophy among its members: Handlers and breeders are encour-

SPRINGER SOUNDBITES

"One of the larger spaniels, this breed has a well-balanced springy body that makes it very attractive. Its charming facial expression makes it a popular domestic dog."
Legacy of the Dog

aged to retain the natural hunting or working instincts of the dog. Breeding strictly for conformation (the show ring) is discouraged. The UKC proudly states that "the majority of the dogs we register still perform the tasks the breeds were originally bred for."

Limited Registration

Many responsible dog owners agree that too many unwanted dogs are dropped off on country roads, taken to animal shelters, or abandoned to roam streets and neighborhoods in search of food, shelter, and companionship. Unfortunately, thousands of dogs are euthanized each year.

In their effort to control the breeding of pet dogs, many breeders today sell pet-quality puppies with a written spay/neuter agreement. The registration papers are withheld until proof of the surgery is received.

AKC's Limited Litter Registration: The dog is registered but cannot be entered in breed competition. Furthermore, no litters produced by that dog are eligible for registration.

Check out those ears.

Even though the spay/neuter agreement could be rescinded by the breeder, many—believing that some puppies are "late bloomers"—hesitated to force such a final decision on their puppies. In January 1990, these breeders, seeking an alternative to the spay/neuter contract, established an AKC procedure for limited registration of litters. Although these puppies themselves are recognized as purebred dogs their offspring cannot be registered.

AKC's Indefinite Listing Privilege (ILP): Perhaps your Springer is purebred but the litter was not registered—the puppies have no "papers." The ILP program is noted for giving purebred dogs a "second chance," allowing unregistered dogs of a registerable breed (like a Springer) to compete in trials.

UKC's Single Registration Privilege: This is not to be confused with the 1991 UKC Limited Privilege Registration Program. In a commendable effort to allow non-purebred dogs to participate in their obedience programs, the UKC offers what it calls single-registration privileges. These dogs must be phenotypically recognizable (that is, they should look like a Beagle, for instance, or look like a Springer) and must be spayed or neutered.

Pedigrees

A pedigree is a written record of Willie's ancestry as recorded in the registration books. We can learn a great deal about our dogs by studying their pedigrees. Even a four-generation pedigree, for instance, contains the full names and titles earned of 30 dogs in your pet's family tree.

How to Read a Pedigree

The term pedigree comes from the French *pied de grue* or "Crane's foot." Apparently, long ago, some inspired researcher decided that the lineage lines of a genealogy chart resembled the spread foot of a crane. As with any effort worth pursuing, it takes some inspiration and a great deal of backup Information to follow through on today's pedigrees. But from a full four-generation pedigree, the patient inquirer can obtain a great deal of knowledge about a puppy's possibilities.

On the top lines a pedigree lists your dog's name, its breed, sex, color, birthdate, and the name of the breeder. The Registration number (a six-digit number with a two-letter prefix) is a source of lifetime identification.

In the body of an AKC certified pedigree, for instance, the four-generation certificate will list similar information for your puppy's parents through their great-great grandparents.

Also listed will be their ancestors' registration numbers, dates of registration, coat color, if requested, and any AKC titles earned. By reading carefully with access to a good breed book, you can determine your dog's most likely good and not-so-good traits. Imagine finding out that one of the top Field Trial winners of all time is in your dog's pedigree! Or maybe you'll find Millie, who was the White House Springer during the first Bush administration!

Traveling with Your Springer

Willie hates to be left at home, and, much preferring to accompany his family on outings, never cares where the car is going, just when. These outings can turn into unpleasant memories unless the dog is well behaved.

What's next?

Car Rides

Begin Willie's training in car courtesy by taking him on short, fun rides. Insist that he occupy the backseat of the car. Never let Willie ride with his head sticking out the window. A flying bug hitting his cornea will cause a lot of pain and possibly cause permanent damage to his sight.

Warning! Because dogs are less and less welcome in our public lives, our pets must occasionally be left unattended in a parked car. In warm weather, if you must leave your dog in the car while you run in for a brief errand, try to park beneath a shade tree. Roll a window down. A car can turn into an oven in a very, very short time. Be sure your errand is indeed brief. Because dogs have few sweat glands they control their body heat with respiration. Consequently, dogs cannot tolerate nearly the amount of heat a human can. With poor ventilation and the lack of oxygen, many pets die needlessly in a closed car. Not sure about it? Put yourself in your dog's place. Pretend you've been left in the car "just for a minute" and someone else is running in "for a minute." Would you be comfortable in the car? Remember that image next time you decide to leave your dog alone.

On Vacation

Depending on how well a dog is trained, it can be pleasant company on a long trip. If you are leaving on vacation and you are sure Willie will be welcome at your destination, by all means bring him along with you. You might want to pack his own food (sometimes the brands you use at home can be difficult to find elsewhere and this is no time to experiment). Be sure his rabies tags are in place and up to date. Be sure your name, home address, and telephone number, or your veterinarian's telephone number, are on his collar. Many owners, seeking a more permanent, visible identification, choose to have their pets tattooed or microchips implanted. The tattoo is etched on the inside of the dog's thigh near his abdomen. The microchip, a tiny transponder about the size of a grain of rice, is placed under loose skin near Willie's shoulder blades. In both cases a national registry retains contact information to help recovery efforts.

Some motels and resorts will accept pets in the room; some have kennel provisions. Check with your travel agent or call before you leave.

If you are traveling in a camper, or tenting, remember that few state or national parks and even fewer private parks allow unleashed pets, so bring along an exercise pen or tie-line for those occasions.

By air: Airline travel with a dog is not complicated, particularly if no plane change is involved, provided that you make your reservations well in advance. Consult your reservation agent for specific travel requirements.

Boarding Your Springer

For some owners, a vacation with a dog is out of the question. Even though European laws are less strict than our own (dogs are often welcome in parks, plazas, restaurants,

Ready to show.

hotels, even at the market), their quarantine laws are not. Your pet could be required to spend weeks at the port of entry waiting for a permit.

In those cases, and other times that are unsuitable, a boarding kennel is a haven. Often part of your veterinarian's services, the kennel is staffed by knowledgeable dog lovers, often the same staff that greets Willie during routine visits. Provide a few favorite toys and leave on vacation content that you have made the right decision.

An equipment box, called a "tack" box by horse and dog folk, holds basic grooming necessities. Some handlers carry their gear in specially designed aluminum cases; others convert wheeled ice coolers; still others search yard sales for old tackle and tool boxes. Whatever your choice for the container, your content options are even more plentiful.

Coat

Medium bristle brush: The silky Springer coat attracts numerous twigs, leaves, and seedlings that nest undiscovered in tangled hair. Getting these released from the tangles can be a chore for both you and your pet. Careful inspection and frequent brushing benefit both of you.

Slicker brush: The bent-wire teeth of this brush, set close together, help remove mats. Slicker brushes will take out large amounts of hair, good if you want to reduce the amount of shedding, not good if you want to keep your dog in show condition.

Wide-tooth comb: The length of the teeth depends on how deep you have to comb or want to comb to reach the dog's undercoat. The teeth of the best combs, those made of stainless steel or chrome-plated brass, have rounded tips that help avoid skin irritation. You may have to experiment.

Trimming

Scissors and strippers: As a novice owner, you should know how to trim the hair from around your pet's eyes and ears, from between his toes, around the bottom of his feet, and around his anus. Stripping, a special grooming technique designed to remove the undercoat from show dogs, is best handled by experienced show professionals.

Nails

Nail clippers: Clipping is not a difficult procedure but it can be anxiety provoking for both of you. It will benefit both of you if you purchase a good pair of guillotine-style clippers. Start nail clipping when your Springer is a puppy.
✔ Sit down with him somewhere with good lighting—outdoors is great.
✔ Hold the puppy's paw.

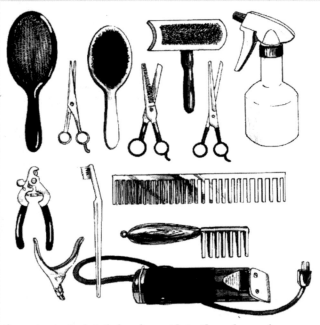

Grooming tools: bristle brushes, wide tooth combs, carders, thinning shears, nail clippers, sprays, and razor.

TACK BOX

✔ Apply a little pressure to push the nail forward.

✔ Clip the tip of one nail—just the tip.

✔ Give the puppy a treat, put him down, and play with him for a minute.

✔ On the second day, proceed in this unhurried manner until he will let you clip one paw with no fuss except wiggly anticipation of a good time with you.

✔ When the two of you sit down to clip all four feet, both of you will know what to expect.

Note: Never clip the "quick" and have styptic powder available should the cut bleed.

Check the nails of indoor pets at least once a month.

Teeth

Toothbrush: The normal Springer has 44 teeth—22 on the top and 22 on the bottom. They should be brushed at least twice a week. Dogs don't normally get cavities but instead form a bacteria-laden brown substance around their gums called calculus. Using a circular motion, specially flavored doggie toothpaste, and a little praise and determination, tooth brushing should not be a chore for either of you. The alternative, a professional scaling and cleaning, involves anesthetizing your pet. Now, wouldn't a little hygienic inconvenience be worth avoiding that alternative?

More Tips

Treats: For those special times when you need a little extra help, keep a special treat bag filled and within easy reach.

Shampoo: Don't leave any soap residue on your dog. A good-quality dog shampoo, while nice to smell, is not as important as a thorough rinse afterward.

Towels: Check out the garage sales. Old beach towels are sized just right for Springers. New beach towels, on sale at the end of the season, are a special bathtime luxury.

FEEDING YOUR SPRINGER

Does your Springer eat the same food that you eat? Ask around and you will discover there are as many different ideas about what to feed your dog as there are products on the shelf.

"Every evening after supper, our dogs, Blondie and Blaze, get a pan of dried dog food mixed with crumbled bread and whatever bones and kitchen scraps I have on hand," one neighbor tells us. "Both dogs are healthy and happy; I'm happy, too, because I don't have any leftovers."

"I buy whatever brand I have a coupon for, or whatever brand is on sale that month," says another neighbor. "I refill a self-feeder twice a week and Rusty eats as much as he wants. He gets plenty of exercise, he's not fat, and this method is a time- and money-saver for me."

The lady from down the street replied, "I buy Duke's food from my veterinarian. We taught him not to beg for snacks, and he doesn't miss them because he's never had them. Yes, it is an expensive diet, but he's worth it."

The neighborhood retiree, queried while walking his pampered pooch, tells us, "My little Magic would rather starve than eat dry dog food. She doesn't even like canned food much,

Yum, yum.

so she eats what we do. I do give her a daily vitamin, though."

Which neighbor is right? Which one is taking better care of a pet? Whom should you believe? What is a new owner to do?

Understanding Canine Nutrition

Each of the neighbors in the story above believes that he or she understands pet nutrition, and each has given some thought to proper feeding. In the light of so many opinions, who can tell which dog owner has the right approach?

Each owner has attempted to provide the necessary nutritional elements while allowing for individual differences and needs on both sides. A little thought, coupled with a reading of some of the following information, should help you to make up your own mind.

We don't have to be nutritionists to feed Tootsie properly. We do, however, need a basic understanding of her needs.

Is that filet mignon I smell?

The Basic Elements

The various state departments of agriculture under the Association of American Feed Control Officials (AAFCO) have established national regulations regarding pet food quality that are required of all pet food manufacturers. In addition, the Pet Food Institute, at the behest of veterinarians, initiated a Nutrition Assurance Program that uses, among other tests, live animal feeding to monitor manufacturer's claims. The result is that if a manufacturers' label, for instance, states that a food is "complete and balanced," and indicates that AAFCO protocols and procedures were followed, you may be sure that the product has been tested and has passed. So, look for the label. If you do feed an AAFCO tested product, be cautious about adding large amounts of kitchen leftovers to your dog's diet. In particular, do not add any

vitamin or mineral supplements unless under the supervision of your veterinarian, as an imbalance could result.

Leading the daily recommendations for a balanced diet are top-quality proteins, carbohydrates, fats, vitamins, minerals, and fresh water, in proper proportion.

These issues are addressed by today's commercial food providers. Once you have decided on a brand, follow the manufacturer's instructions as to age and formula requirements. You and Tootsie will be glad you did.

Types of Dog Food

It really is a matter of personal preference (yours and Tootsie's) and a matter of economics (yours) as to which type of food you feed her as long as that choice contains the proper nutritional levels. The following information may help you reach a decision on feeding.

Canned Food

Canned dog food is cooked, sterile, and convenient. If the label states that the food is nutritionally balanced, such a diet will provide all the necessary nutrients for your pet. About 50 percent of the protein in canned products comes from meat, poultry, or fish products. The remaining protein usually is derived from eggs or dried milk. Dried skim milk and dried buttermilk are common additions. One can of food contains about 450 calories with the carbohydrates provided by corn, barley, or wheat.

Many owners, when comparing packaged and dry dog food with the more costly canned food, find that the latter smells more appealing and looks more realistic than the first two. Although aware that they are paying a premium price for the can's water content, many owners—particularly of smaller breeds—feed canned food exclusively. Economically, this option often is not available to owners of medium or large breeds.

Semimoist Food

The semimoist dog foods, usually wrapped in cellophane packages, contain half the water of canned food. Because they need no refrigeration, even when opened, semimoist packages are convenient for travelers or vacationers. If you do plan to use these products as a convenience when traveling, be aware that a sudden change in diet can upset your dog's digestive system. It is best to introduce the change gradually while on home grounds.

A 6-ounce (170 g) pouch or patty contains the equivalent calorie count to a 1-pound (454-g) can of dog food. Although these packaged foods may look like burgers, they are, unlike canned products, relatively odorless, and thus may be unappetizing.

Dry Food

Bagged, loose-pack dry foods are usually granulated, pelleted or flaked, then homogenized and cooked. Each flake or pellet contains a mix of meat meals, grain, and vegetable products. Depending on the brand, certain vitamin and mineral supplements are added to bring the product up to AAFCO standards.

Homemade Food

Although AAFCO-approved commercial dog foods guarantee a balanced diet, many pet owners consider, at one time or another, home-

Waiting patiently.

made feeding. Owners of kitchen-raised litters, or orphaned puppies, for instance, often provide special diets for the newcomers.

It is important that the homemade diet follow the proper nutritional guidelines as closely as possible. For puppies, that balance should be close to 25 percent protein, 25 percent fat, and 50 percent carbohydrates. Cooked or dry cereal, cooked rice or toast, and cooked hamburger

While waiting.

are good starter possibilities. Milk, meat broth, or warm water can be added as necessary. Vegetable oil and vitamin and mineral supplements also can be added as necessary.

Additives and Supplements

Your pet requires vitamins A, D, E, and K as well as vitamin B, niacin, and folic acid just as we do. (Vitamin C is not a recognized dietary requirement for dogs.) Commercial foods labeled as complete or balanced supply adequate amounts of these supplements.

Remember to be careful with dietary supplements. Even adding vitamins and minerals to an already balanced diet can result in serious nutritional deficiencies. Other problems can be caused by erroneous assumptions about a dog's needs. Meat, for instance, is an important part of Tootsie's diet, but an all-meat diet is not nutritionally balanced.

Bones and Biscuits

Baked dog bones and biscuits are made by mixing wheat or soybean flour with meat meal, milk products, and vitamin and mineral supplements. The resulting dough is cut into shapes and baked.

Dogs love these starchy treats. They make handy snacks and even handier training helpers. If your pet is overweight, remember to count calories when assessing his diet. Each bone in a nationally advertised, standard size "flavor snack," for instance, contains about 20 calories.

Healthy puppies eat, sleep, eat, play, eat, tussle, and eat some more.

Feeding Facts

Same Time, Same Place

Dogs appreciate consistency. Because meal-time is often the highlight of Tootsie's day, it would make sense to feed her a fixed, stable diet on a regular schedule.

Some owners successfully introduce a self-feeding schedule that allows the dog to eat from a dispenser-type container filled with dry dog food. Tootsie can consume as much or as little as she likes. Proponents of self-feeding note several advantages:

✔ Primarily the dog does not have to wait for her supper if her family is late returning from work.

✔ A dog that nibbles throughout the day maintains a constant level of nutrients in her body.

✔ Constant nibbling reduces that before-meal-time excitement that can cause digestive upsets.

Begging and Other Bad Habits

Begging is cute when it is part of a repertoire of tricks, but begging at the dinner table is not socially acceptable. Trying to teach a frisky Springer to beg only when family is present is more than most Springers can comprehend; better not to start the habit at all. The Monks of New Skete, widely praised for their dog-training methods, allow their dogs to accompany them to the dining hall. Each animal lies quietly until its master is finished, not leaving its place until given a command.

Finicky Eaters

Most dog behaviorists believe that dogs are trained by us to be picky about the foods they eat. Remember the puppy rule that says, "Feed

B.A.R.F.

Proponents of the Biologically Appropriate Raw Food (BARF) diet, also known as the Bones and Raw Food diet, are convinced that serving homemade, handmade food is the key to having a healthier dog.

Enthusiasts, opposed to feeding their dogs processed, canned, and pelleted foods, offer, among other choices, raw chicken wings, raw, meaty bones, whole fish, rabbit, boiled eggshells, table scraps, and similar foods.

A trip to the vegetable market for sweet potatoes, broccoli, apples (remove the seeds before feeding), turnip greens, and carrots, with a stop for yogurt and cottage cheese, provides a base for the BARF dinner. Coupled with a pound of ground lamb, chicken, beef, or turkey, and spiced with a little honey, garlic, or an egg, Tootsie's dinners will be fit for a queen, or at least as fit as her master's.

Note that the BARF grocery list does not include grains or complex carbohydrates. Dogs are carnivores. Like wolves, dogs do not have the digestive system to handle cereal such as corn, wheat, rice, and soy.

Whatever feeding method you select, watch your pet closely. Add new foods gradually. If Tootsie shows signs of gas, diarrhea, or vomiting, remove the offending food from her diet immediately.

a puppy up to its appetite." Tootsie will eat when she is hungry. Your responsibility is to train her to be hungry when you fill her food bowl. If your dog has not finished her meal in 30 minutes, pick up her bowl. At the next normal feeding, fill the bowl as usual and set it out again. When attempting to set up a feed-

ing schedule, don't allow the dog to have
snacks between feedings.

Feeding by Age and Activity Level

Your pet's nutritional needs change as she
matures. Amounts and times of feeding also
depend on activity, climate, and physical condition. Young puppies, for instance, must be fed
four to five times a day. The following
information should help you to determine a
proper feeding schedule for your dog.

Mmm-mmm good.

Puppies Under Six Months of Age

A workable feeding schedule for a two- to
three-month-old puppy is 7:00 A.M., Noon, 5:00
P.M., and 10:00 P.M. At this age offer the puppy
a commercially mixed dry dog food, developed
specifically for puppies, mixed with slightly
warm water if you like.

At age three months most puppies can
sleep happily all night without the help of
the 10:00 P.M. feeding. For the first few mornings after eliminating the night feeding,
however, be prepared to offer breakfast a
little earlier.

By the time the puppy is four months old
her permanent teeth will begin to erupt. For
the next three months, these itchy gums
prompt the puppy to chew on almost anything.
Dry crunchy dog food is preferred by this age
group. Chew toys and bones (not poultry
bones!) offer some relief for aching gums.

Puppies Under One Year of Age

Puppies at the age of six months are enter-
ing into an active period of fully charged adolescence. Their protein and carbohydrate needs
are high. Six- to 12-month-old puppies spend
less time sleeping and expend more energy
investigating their world. Meals can be cut
down to twice a day. Six or seven months of
age is also a good time to try self-feeding,
which allows the puppy to adjust her intake as
needed. Be careful that she doesn't get too fat.
If she can't discipline herself as she self-feeds,
go back to twice-a-day feeding.

Adult Dog

By the time Tootsie is 15 to 18 months old
she will have reached a level of maturity that
allows you to once more make changes in her

A nice nap after dinner.

diet. If you have not adopted self-feeding, continue a twice-a-day feeding schedule but change to a commercial diet that contains maintenance level proteins balanced for adult dogs. Tootsie herself may cut down to eating once a day. You will know when this happens, of course, because one meal will be left virtually uneaten. Try to follow her lead on this.

Pregnant and Nursing Bitches

The stress of pregnancy can take a toll on your dog's energy and health. It is extremely important to feed a pregnant bitch a diet higher in protein than usual. Many breeders return to puppy formulas because of this added need. Toward the end of her pregnancy, perhaps as soon as the seventh week, your dog may be too uncomfortable to eat large meals. You can help by offering smaller meals several times a day, or by providing a self-feeder.

After the litter arrives, the puppies receive nourishment from their mother for three to four weeks. This added burden on her system puts the mother under great nutritional stress. She will require more than twice the normal

TIP

Water

The most important supplement you can give your pet is fresh water. Water is required for all normal cell functions. Because water is not stored in the body but is excreted, a ready supply of fresh water should be available at all times.

Somebody call dinner?

amounts of food. Here, too, a self-feeding system works well.

Older Dogs

Less energy leads to longer naps and a more sedentary lifestyle. A drop in activity allows extra calories to add pounds to a once handsome body.

Worn or missing teeth can also cause problems. If your pet has trouble eating dry food, make an appointment with your veterinarian for a dental checkup. Meanwhile, try softening that food in warm water as you did when your dog was a puppy.

Overweight Dogs

Lowering Tootsie's fat intake while monitoring her caloric intake can add quality time to her life. Veterinarians tell us that more than 50 percent of the general dog population is overweight. Once again, as responsible owners, we can put our dogs on a diet easier than we can diet ourselves. Tootsie cannot open the pantry door and help herself to the cookies. Count every calorie, if necessary with the help of one of the low-calorie commercial foods. Increase her exercise level. Tootsie will appreciate it and will look better and live longer.

What Not to Feed Your Pet

"My dog is so fat he waddles. He can't help it that he loves fudge ripple ice cream. It's gotten so bad he won't let me eat until I give him a bowl, too," sighs one friend.

"When we go to the drive-in for lunch," adds another dog lover, "I order two burgers and two fries, one bag for me and one for my dog, Charlie."

"Once or twice a week, Buster and I sit down in front of the TV and chow down on a bag of chocolate bells," says another. "He loves them as much as I do."

What's wrong here? Are these pets loved or spoiled? As a pet owner you have a responsibility to see that your pet eats the right foods

TIP

Don't Feed!
✔ Chocolate, cola, and tea contain theobromine, a compound similar to caffeine. The amount that could cause seizures, coma, and even death depends on the size of the dog and the amount ingested. Best to stay away from these treats altogether.
✔ Fish, chicken, or pork bones can shatter whether raw or cooked. Leave them alone and give Tootsie a chew toy.
✔ Walnuts, particularly those already on the ground, may contain a toxic mold. Keep an eye on your dog as you walk through the park.
✔ Fried and fatty foods, cakes, pies, and desserts are just plain not good for your pet, and kernels of whole corn are indigestible.
✔ Seed those apples. Apple seeds contain cyanide.

Let's go for a walk.

and stays away from the wrong ones. Particularly if your Springer is overweight, or has special dietary needs, you must take charge of her diet.

Regardless of her weight, don't feed your Springer:
✔ fried foods
✔ chocolate
✔ kernels of whole corn
✔ raw egg whites
✔ cakes
✔ pies
✔ desserts
✔ fish, chicken, or pork bones

Ignore Tootsie's longing looks, sad eyes, and appealing gaze directed at a food that is not good for her. Instead, distract her with an offer of a more nourishing snack. Even though you are eating fried chips, Tootsie will be just as happy with a dog biscuit or a bit of cheese if she also receives your attention, a pat on the head, and a word of praise.

PUPPY KINDERGARTEN

Puppy discipline begins in puppyhood. A puppy, if not trained by his master, soon decides to train himself. The results aren't pretty.

Living with a dog trained to respond on command can be one of life's great pleasures. Living with a dog that ignores instructions or one that obeys occasionally can be a nightmare that can only get worse with time. The untrained dog is a nuisance to you and his neighborhood and a hazard to himself.

The training suggestions in this chapter are particularly useful for puppies three to seven months old. Wait to begin serious obedience training until your puppy is able to understand and respond to simple training routines. For most puppies, that understanding comes around the sixth or seventh month of life. Before that time, the puppy's enthusiasm will get in the way of his learning and you will both be discouraged. From three to six or seven months, teach puppy games, puppy kindergarten training, and puppy love.

A puppy, if not trained by his master, soon decides to train himself. That self-training is usually not what you had in mind. It is much

Good friends.

more difficult to teach *"Yes"* and *"No"* to an animal that has already decided to ignore *"No."* Even when properly trained, dogs reach a period of adolescent rebelliousness at about seven to nine months of age. Routines done to perfection one week are wildly imaginative the next. Just push through. Understanding will come.

Guidelines

Here are five basic guidelines:

1. Be observant. Not all Springers respond in the same way to training. Take a long look at any previous training attempts, your dog's attitude, his preferences, his daily routines, and his willingness to please. Naturally willing, some Springers have too much instinctive eagerness pushing them to be on the trail, so to speak, before they are ready for the journey.

2. Be patient. Likely, the procedures are new for both of you. Just remember, when working with your pet, give both corrections and rewards immediately to ensure that the puppy links his infraction or his good behavior with your resulting reaction.

3. Have fun. Don't be harsh or vindictive even when aggravated beyond endurance. Make your corrections firmly but gently. If necessary, abandon the session. Start over again the next day, opening with a command your pet has mastered. Proceed from that command with a smile and the authority of one who cares.

4. Trainers agree that the adage "Practice makes perfect" is only partly correct. The motto should be "Perfect practice makes perfect." Perfect practice is setting up regular training times—before meals is best—and sticking to them. Perfect practice time is fun. If you enjoy yourself, your dog will have a good time, too. What is more, he will learn more quickly and look forward to working out with you. Perfect practice is teaching simple lessons and practicing them over and over again.

Obedience is a direct result of good communication which is a direct result of close companionship.

5. Don't expect miracles. Keep in mind that if your dog understands what you expect and, if at the same time, he wants to please you, he will react as you wish.

Basic Training

Teaching a dog to understand what you want of him may be one of the hardest jobs you have ever attempted. Some pets and their masters never learn to communicate. When you both finally break through the barrier you can be justly proud of your accomplishments.

How and Why Springers Learn

Animal behaviorists tell us that our dogs learn by associating an action with a result. That is why immediate reaction on your part is so important. Correct or praise immediately after the fact. If you feel you are being forced to give an inappropriate amount of correction, try to prevent a misdeed in the first place. Try not to give a command that will not be obeyed. Don't give a *"Come!"* for instance, unless your puppy is on leash and you can coerce him to come if he doesn't come willingly. Don't give an *"Off!"* or a *"Fetch"* or a *"Down"* unless you are prepared to follow through.

Take advantage of the fact that Springers naturally like to be with and to please their masters. They are at our side when we walk, at our feet when we sit down. They seem to ask little from us but our attention and sometimes not even that. Our presence is sufficient. When we try to leave them behind we are treated to the saddest and most reproachful eyes in creation.

Springers enjoy being useful. Bred to work, to hunt, to accompany their masters in the field, and curious by nature, Springers can become so agitated at the prospect of a walk in unexplored country that unless leashed they will bound from the car, propelled by new aromas and new fields to conquer. A Springer can be so stimulated the night before a trip by the sight of hunting gear taken from the closet and put in the car that he is physically unable to sleep.

We are told that dogs have no sense of the future, do not understand our motivations, do not understand our language, and never will. They, nevertheless,

✔ do remember people and experiences in total detail

✔ do recognize tones of voice and facial expressions

✔ do understand kindness and respond to it with obedience and lifelong devotion.

Use this hard-earned knowledge when you work with your dog.

Who's the Boss?

Some behavior is instinctive, bred into your dog through the years to produce certain traits. Some German Shepherd Dogs are bred to be guard dogs. Some Spaniels are bred to be companionable lapdogs. Your Springer possesses a basic instinct for hunting that helps him to be a better bird dog than a Dalmatian, a better swimmer than a Chihuahua, and a faster runner than a Dachshund. Yet, all of these dogs—the German Shepherd, the Spaniel, the Dalmatian, the Chihuahua, and the Dachshund—share one basic instinct. None of these dogs will willingly live alone. Each has a need to be part of a pack. When you take a puppy away from his natural relatives and introduce him to your own family, that family becomes his pack.

SPRINGER SOUNDBITES

"The Golden Rule of dog training is simple. For each 'question' (command), there is only one correct 'answer' (reaction). Keep practicing the command until the dog reacts correctly without hesitating. Be repetitive but not monotonous."
Charlotte Schwartz, trainer

When training and working with your Springer, you should remember two important aspects of pack behavior:

1. Each pack has one leader.

2. There is no such position as co-leader. You either are the boss or you are not. When you and your Springer train, one of you will be the leader. It is up to you to assume the role.

Are you coming?

Using a Choke Chain Collar

✔ Attach the leash to the collar.
✔ Hold the free ring of the collar in your left hand.
✔ Using your right hand, pick up the hanging chain of the collar and drop a section of the chain (with the leash still attached) through the free ring. Widen the resulting circle.
✔ Face your dog. Hold the collar and leash so that the shape resembles a capital letter "P" with the leash on the left, forming the stem of the "P."
✔ Pull the choke collar over your dog's head letting the leash fall free down the right side of the dog's neck.
✔ Adjust the collar so that it sits high on your dog's neck, just behind the ears. Check the position by giving a strong pull on the leash. If the collar is properly set it will tighten immediately and loosen as immediately when you release the pressure. This is very important. The choke collar must hang free when the dog is performing as expected. An improperly applied collar, one that is always tight, is of no use in training.

As leader, your first job is to be certain your dog obeys every command you give. Insist on obedience. Don't give a command unless you can reinforce it. If you find you have to physically put the dog in a *"Down,"* for instance, don't hesitate to do so. For most of us, this means working on a leash until you are sure the dog will obey.

Your Training Tools

Basically, you will use four tools: two collars and two leashes. A flat collar and basic 6-foot (2 m) leash are used for everyday handling. A metal slip-chain collar is added during training sessions. A 20- to 30-foot long (6–10 m) leash or line is indispensable for controlling your pet when out-of-doors, teaching *"Come,"* for instance.

Dog Collars

By the time Sandy has completed his basic puppy shots (at about four months of age) you will surely want him to be accustomed to a collar. Your veterinarian probably has a supply and can make a recommendation. Flat, buckled collars are easily sized. Try one on your dog. If you can slip three fingers between your pet's neck and the collar, it is sized just right. Check the fit often because the growing puppy will outgrow the collar before you know it. Flat nylon webbed or lightweight leather collars are inexpensive and appropriate for puppies.

A lightweight slip-chain metal training collar, commonly called a choke chain collar, will be one of your most valuable training tools. The common name "choke" is misleading. Properly used, the collar will not choke your pet but will get his attention. The collar could properly be called a check collar because the purpose is to check (stop) an activity. Be sure to remove the collar after each session and replace it with a flat, buckled collar. Free-running pets have been strangled when choke chain collars catch on fences, branches, or other obstacles in the field.

Leash

Metal leashes are often too heavy for a young Springer. Either a leather or a webbed leash about 6 feet (2 m) long is satisfactory. Because some leather leashes are also too heavy and because the webbed leashes are light and colorful, the latter are often first choice.

To hold the leash correctly, put your right thumb through the loop. Fold and keep a tight hold of all but an arm's length of leash in your right hand. (The leash comes out of your grasp near your little finger.) Place your left hand on the leash immediately next to your right hand. If the collar rings are together and the leash snap is hanging down, the leash is on correctly. Hold your elbows close to your body slightly below waist level.

Whistle

Many trainers cultivate a whistle to call in their dogs. Those unable to summon a loud enough whistle often purchase slim silver-toned whistles and hang them around their necks at training times. Used mostly in conjunction with the *"Come"* command, the whistle can be a very helpful training adjunct.

Click, Treat. Click, Treat. Click, Treat

Clicker training is a useful tool for you and your pet. The sound is unique and therefore interesting. The addition of a food treat will encourage your dog to pay attention. When your dog looks at the clicker and then at you, he is beginning to understand that "click" means treat. Turn this learned behavior into a skill. Click every time the dog does something you want him to do. For instance, give the verbal command *"Shake."* When he does, click and give a treat.

Food as Reward

You are trying to train your dog that a command from you requires a certain action on his

Waiting for the word.

part. When your pet acts appropriately, be quick with a positive response. Although several well-respected trainers insist that a dog must work for a kind word alone, there is nothing basically wrong with offering your dog a treat for a job well done. Bites of liver, dog biscuits, and cheese are rewards that, when offered at the proper time, help you to say "Good job." When reinforced by verbal praise, playtime, hugs, and pats, food treats become a part of positive motivation. Your dog will learn that love, discipline, and treats all come from the same source.

A problem arises when the concept of a special reward is carried too far and the treat is

TIP

Treat Recipe

One recipe that has proven a favorite on the show and training circuit follows:

8 oz. (1 kg) beef liver
2 tsp. (10 g) garlic powder
1 tsp. (5 g) salt
2 cups (235 ml) water

Dice liver into 1/2-inch (1 cm) cubes. Add salt and garlic powder and liver to the water. Bring water mixture to a rolling boil. Reduce heat and simmer 25 minutes or until the liver is fork tender. Remove from heat, drain, and cool. Refrigerate. Will keep up to two weeks.

both anticipated and expected. Because there will be many times when you want your dog to obey without any incentive except a desire to please you, be sure your puppy receives plenty of hugs and verbal praise, too.

Playtime, quiet time, school time. Spend quality time with your friend.

On the subject of treats, showdogs are selected partly for their conformation (how good they look) and partly for their enthusiasm. That enthusiasm is often enhanced by treats offered by a handler. Watch the eyes of a showdog sparkle as he anticipates a bit of liver. Watch closely at the next conformation show. Savvy handlers keep these boiled treats at instant readiness hidden in their jacket pockets, folded into a long sleeve, or tucked like snuff into their own cheeks.

Voice and Body Signals

Many of us believe a properly motivated Springer puppy can understand many more words than was once thought. It is known that an adult Springer can respond to at least 20 command words. It is important that these words be short, positive, and distinguishable. Avoid using the same word for two situations. This happens most frequently with the command word *"Down."* If you use *"Down"* to mean *"Lie down on the floor,"* don't use *"Down"* when you want your puppy off the sofa or to stop jumping on people, for instance. The commands *"Off!"* and *"No jumping!"* work well for those situations.

The five most frequently used commands are referred to as the mantra of basic obedience. These five commands are *"Sit," "Come," "Stay," "Heel,"* and *"Down."* For best results, don't use these command words for any situation other than to initiate basic obedience routines.

In addition to the mantra of five, other commands your Springer can learn to respond to are *"Watch," "Enough," "Okay," "No more," "Off," "Give," "Drop it," "Good," "Move," "Out," "Take it," "Leave it," "Jump in," "No*

Sit! Good boy! Watch me!

jumping," "Kennel up," "Let's go," "Hurry up," and *"Wait."*

To release your dog from any command, give him a couple of quick pats on the chest and a warm *"Okay!"*

Tone of Voice

Your dog connects the words you say with your body language and the tone of your voice in order to understand your meaning. Voice change is natural. Most animal lovers change their tone of voice when speaking to a favorite pet. They have learned that intimate, crooning tones, for instance, cause their pet's ears to perk up. Often that pet will sit, head cocked to one side, as he listens.

Successful dog handlers cultivate two distinct changes of tone when speaking to a dog. Praise is best offered in a happy, loving, singsong tone of voice quite unlike a normal speaking voice. Corrections are given in a stern, no-nonsense tone of final authority. Whether you are teaching the official obedience commands or one of those designed to make everyday living more comfortable, cultivate your own training voices. Practice those voices until they become natural to you.

Body Language

When you praise your Springer, be happy and be sure you convey that happiness to your pet. Some trainers jump up and down, others clap their hands and applaud enthusiastically. Others offer a treat for a job well done and give their pet a pat on the head and a rub under the chin.

On the other hand, when their pets must be disciplined, these savvy trainers have learned to

turn away, avert their eyes, correct their dogs in a low, disappointed tone of voice or even a growl.

Teaching Basic Obedience in Six Weeks

Some dog owners say that if their dog just learns to come when called, they will be satisfied. Actually, though, because the obedience commands are built on a structure, each reinforces the other. *"Come"* is one of the most difficult commands to teach. *"Sit,"* on the other hand, can be taught to puppies three months old and even younger.

"Sit"

"Sit," a useful, easy-to-learn command, is known as the attention-getting command. Your dog learns to sit while anticipating the next command.

Hold the leash in your right hand close to the collar and put your Springer on your left

Heel! Good boy! Keep your head even with my left knee!

side. You will be standing next to your dog with both of you facing straight ahead. Say *"Sit."* (Do not use your dog's name.) Simultaneously pull up on the leash with your right hand and stroke the dog's back with your left hand, eventually pushing down on the dog's hindquarters if necessary. When your dog sits, pet him and praise him. Invite him to play for a minute or two before going on to another lesson or before trying that one again. "What a

SPRINGER SOUNDBITES

"To obtain proper response and avoid confusion a trainer should always use the exact same commands to direct and control his dog."
Ernie Wunderlich, trainer

good dog! You are the best puppy! I never had such a wonderful puppy!"

The puppy should hold a *sit* position for several seconds before being released with an *"Okay."* If he starts to move before the *"Okay,"* say *"No!"* and pull up on the leash. Wait several more seconds, give an *"Okay"* and praise your pet. Give him a treat at this time if you like.

Within a day or two you won't have to push on the dog's hindquarters any longer. Instead, you can use your left hand to teach the hand signal for *"Sit"*: Extend your left arm straight in front of you, above your dog's eye level. Point your index finger toward your pet while saying *"Sit."*

"Heel"

An aimless stroll on a starry night, or a walk off leash through the woods or field on a wonderfully sunny day can be heaven for you and your dog. But because most of our dog walking is on a busy street or in a town or neighborhood with strict leash laws, we can't walk off leash as often as we would like. One of the benefits of teaching our pets to enjoy walking at heel is that even when walking on leash we can offer them as much of that sense of companionship and freedom as possible.

First, sit your dog at your left side (the *heel* position), his head even with your left knee. Attach the leash and the choke chain. Hold the leash in your right hand. Call your dog's name. Say, *"Sandy, heel."* At that same moment, start off on your left foot. Pat your leg. Move briskly. Keep the lead as short and slack as possible.

Be enthusiastic. Assume Sandy will want to come walking with you. Keep up a stream of animated patter: "Good boy, aren't we having fun? Sandy's a good dog! Look at us go! Let's

CHECKLIST

Commands

When teaching these commands, follow six guidelines:

✔ Work on the commands in the order listed: *"Sit," "Heel," "Stay," "Come,"* and *"Down."* Work on one new command a week. Each week add the next command and review the previous commands.

✔ Hold training sessions five or fewer days a week, twice a day for 15 to 20 minutes each time. Have fun.

✔ To be sure your dog will obey you, begin each of these commands with your pet on a leash. Don't attempt any of these off leash until you are confident you will be obeyed.

✔ Correct your dog before he has a chance to disobey or ignore you. Some trainers jump in and correct if they even suspect a problem of inattention.

✔ Precede the moving commands (*"Down"* and *"Heel"*) with your dog's name. When you give a stationary command (*"Sit," "Stay,"* and *"Down"*), omit your dog's name. Thus you would say, *"Sandy, heel!"* or *"Sandy, come!"* but *"Stay."*

✔ This last suggestion is difficult to follow, but very important. DON'T REPEAT A COMMAND. Your dog heard you the first time. Once is enough. If your dog hasn't responded, go to the dog and physically make him obey (push on him, pull him, lift him, lure him, whatever) without giving the command a second time. The idea behind this rule is that you don't want Sandy to decide to wait for time number three, or to wait until a certain amount of growling and exasperation enters your voice. If growling is what it takes to make your dog obey, rethink your training voice. Sound exasperated the first time.

go walking, you and me, just a bit more, good boy, here we go." Walk in a straight line. Your puppy will be excited and will forge ahead to investigate new smells or will head out on his own exploration and veer into you. Just nudge him over, keep on walking, talk to him to keep him interested. For the first lessons, you're both doing fine if you can walk at least ten paces without generating any leash tension.

If you have to correct your puppy, and you will, correct quickly with a short, downward snap on the leash. "Check, release, and praise," my first teacher said. "Be quick about it, snap and release." In other words, make the correction and keep on walking. Sandy will look up at you as if to ask if you felt that sudden pull, too. Act as if you had nothing to do with that momentary tightening of the collar around his neck. He will figure out that when he doesn't pay attention, something strange happens. When Sandy does watch you, you make him feel good. Walk on, talking to him: "Good boy, that's the way, come on, Sandy, let's go as far as that tree. Come on, now, let's go. Here we go, good boy."

"Stay" right here and wait for me.

In later lessons, practice turning, circling, cornering, and walking among other dogs and people. Always practice on leash. Don't move to off leash until you are confident your puppy will follow your every step and that may take months. You may be sure that if Sandy won't walk under control on a loose leash he is not ready for off-leash heeling. Even then, carry the leash with you to slip back on at the first sign of insurrection.

"Stay"

Once again, sit your puppy on your left, in *heel* position, both of you facing straight ahead. Hold a tight leash in your left hand. Now bring your right hand in front of your dog's face (like a traffic patrolman's "Stop" signal) and push that hand, palm forward, toward the puppy, saying, *"Stay!"* Using your right foot, step out and stop directly in front of your dog. Which foot you use to step out with is an

important point, because your pet should be watching your left foot expecting a signal to heel. Keep your eye on your dog, count to ten, and then step back to the *heel* position. Release the pressure on the leash, say *"Okay,"* and praise your puppy. Praise him whether he really did okay or not. You may have had to return to your dog once or twice to reinforce the command, but in the end, before the lesson was concluded, he did stay, so praise joyously. Release your dog. Play games. Throw a stick down the path. Race to see who gets to the stick first. (You lose.) Have fun. Smile and laugh and be enthusiastic. Speak warmly to your dog: "Good boy, Sandy, good job! What a good time we are having!" (If you get even a 30-second *stay* at this point in your training you both deserve some fun time.)

For the next lesson, still on leash, gradually increase the distance between you and your puppy. Move back, perhaps 3 feet (91 cm) this time, and again give the command *"Stay!"* If that works as you expect it to, move 6 feet (183 cm) farther away the following week and try again. Remember, when your puppy does as you command, be ready with hugs and pats and praise. Eventually, maybe next week, maybe the week after that, if all is progressing nicely, try *"Stay"* without the leash. Be ready, though, to step in with a correction the moment your dog even glances away.

Remember that the purpose of *"Stay"* is to get your dog to wait for you, so if he moves or if you even think he is about to move, step right in with a firm correction. Say *"No! Stay!"* in a stern tone.

By the end of six weeks your dog should stay off leash at least six minutes. Eventually, you can work up to moving out of sight, or going into the house for a few minutes and expecting your puppy to stay. The dog won't be thrilled, but he is able to stay and he should.

"Come"

The fun command, *"Come"* is called the command that must be obeyed. *"Come"* also must be learned on leash. If your puppy learns that he can disobey *"Come,"* you will have a difficult time enforcing it later. Precede the command with your dog's name, as you did with *"Heel."*

The whistle signal for *"Come"* is a series of beep-beep-beeps. Start whistling immediately after you give the command and continue the whole time the dog is coming toward you.

Because *"Come"* is a command that must be obeyed, make that command attractive. Try kneeling down and clapping your hands. Hold your arms out as a welcome. Hug your dog when he arrives, give him lots of praise and a really tasty treat. When you are training for *"Come,"* always have a pat, a kind word, a treat, or all three for that happy puppy. Make that puppy believe that coming to you is much more fun than not coming.

Two very important points about "Come" training:

1. Never correct or discipline your dog after he has finally come. The dog will not understand the correction. In his mind, he came to you and you fussed at him.

2. Never ignore your Springer when he comes to you following a *come* command. Pat him, hug him, talk to him, give him a good rub under the chin or between the ears, and make him happy that he came.

Wait for me.

"Down"

Some Springers have a difficult time with *"Down"* because it is against their nature to be subservient. Because you are expecting to see some form of subservience, don't let the *down* command become a battle of wills unless you plan to win.

Again, this command is learned on leash. Put Sandy in the *sit* position. Hold the leash in your left hand leaving several feet of the leash still on the floor. Move out with your right foot until you are standing in front of the puppy. Once again, bring your right hand in front of your dog's face (remember the traffic patrolman's "Stop" signal) but this time as you give the *down* command, move your hand down toward the floor. Say *"Dow-n-n-n."*

There are several good methods for teaching *"Down."* Select one and be ready to try another if that doesn't work. Primarily, you are trying to lure your dog to associate an action with a command. You might carefully pull Sandy's

front paws forward, while pushing on his shoulders, thereby forcing him into a prone position. Experiment with the command. Be careful with this command. Don't get very loud and annoyed; don't get very forceful with the pressure. You don't want to frighten your dog. Be gentle, be aware, and offer plenty of praise and affection. Soon enough your dog will learn *"Down"* and you will both have progressed nicely in your training.

The Canine Good Citizen Award

In an effort to stem the American public's increasing unhappiness with stray, untrained, and unreliable neighborhood dogs, some responsible trainers devised a course designed to produce a Canine Good Citizen (CGC).

The course, offered over a period of six to eight weeks, is usually sponsored by local all-breed clubs, humane societies, and 4-H Clubs.

Canine College: Retrieving a pheasant dummy.

The lessons, often held in neighborhood parks, on school playgrounds, and in shopping centers, conclude with a ten-point test designed to measure the dog's basic manners. Those dogs passing the test receive a certificate certifying that they demonstrated appropriate behavior in public with people and with other dogs. The program has received great public acceptance and its graduates are recognized by many organizations. Therapy Dogs International, for instance, will not accept a dog for further training until it is CGC-certified.

In CGC training, dogs are required to earn a passing grade for each of the following requirements:

Station 1: Accepting a friendly stranger: The evaluator, ignoring the dog, walks up to the handler and offers a friendly greeting. The dog must not show any discomfort, and must not break position.

Station 2: Sitting politely for petting: The evaluator pets the dog on the head and body. Again, the dog must not show any resentment or shyness.

Station 3: Appearance or grooming: The evaluator inspects the dog to see if he is clean and well groomed. The dog must appear to be healthy, with proper weight and appearance. The evaluator softly brushes the dog's coat, lightly examines the ears, and gently picks up each front foot.

Station 4: Out for a walk: The evaluator will call out a right turn, a left turn, and an about turn with at least one stop in between.

Station 5: Walking through a crowd: The dog must pass close to several people. He may show some interest in the others but must continue to walk with the handler and must not strain on leash.

First lessons in retrieving.

Station 6: Sit and Down on command and staying in place: This station will provide a 20-foot (6 m) leash. The handler puts the dog in a *sit* or *down*. The handler then commands the dog to *"Stay,"* turns, and walks the length of the leash.

Station 7: Coming when called: The handler walks 10 feet (3 m) from the dog, turns to face the dog, and calls him to come.

Station 8: Reaction to another dog: Two handlers and their dogs approach each other from a distance of about 10 feet (3 m), stop, shake hands, and continue on for about 10 feet. Neither dog should go to the other dog or its handler.

Station 9: Reaction to distraction: The evaluator will present two distractions such as dropping a chair, a crutch, or a cane, rolling a crate dolly past the dog, or having a jogger run in front of the dog. The dog should not panic, try to run away, show aggression, or bark.

Station 10: Supervised separation: Evaluators will say something like, "Would you like me to watch your dog?" and take hold of the dog's leash. The owner will go out of sight for three minutes. The dog should not bark, whine, pace, or be extremely agitated or nervous.

Teaching Livable, Practical Habits

There is no secret to teaching a dog to obey, and there is only one rule: Be sure you and your dog are speaking the same language. Each of the following commands is a common sense procedure. Be sure your puppy is ready to learn and play before you start.

"Leave It"

When you want your puppy to drop an object he is carrying or to cease investigating an intriguing odor, use *"Leave it."* This command is also appropriate when you want your puppy to wait for permission to accept a treat instead of lunging for it. Put your dog in a *sit* using the left-hand index finger as a reminder. Say sternly, *"Leave it!"* Remove the object with your hand and drop it to the ground. Do not let the dog pick it up again until you release him with a quick *"Okay!"*

"Give"

When you want your dog to place an object in your hand, a stick or glove he has retrieved, for instance, hold out your hand and say *"Give!"* Take the object from the dog if necessary by tapping him lightly under the chin. Don't get into a tug of war.

Be careful with *"Give."* Don't use the command every single time the puppy retrieves. Puppies tire easily, and they particularly hate to hand over their hard-won treasures. Allow

Canine College: Learning to negotiate an A-Frame.

your puppy to run off and snuggle down with his treasure occasionally.

"Off"

When you want your pet off the sofa or off your easy chair, or to stop jumping on you, remember not to use the command *"Down."* Save this important command for "lie down on the floor," or "lie down and wait for me." Substitute *"Off!"* instead of *"Down"* for "get off the chair." If necessary—and it will be necessary in the beginning—give the command, and when your puppy stares at you like you must be mistaken, help him off the sofa. The moment all four feet are on the floor, praise your dog for following orders. Help the puppy find a place to lie down that is equally (well,

almost) comfortable and more acceptable. A floor pillow, a rug behind the chair, or his own crate are good alternates.

"Hurry Up"

Some dog owners have tried to find another phrase for their dog's act of elimination instead of "let's go potty," "do your business," or "time to tinkle." Your dog doesn't particularly care which words you use—or which language you use, for that matter. (I had some Shar-pei friends who knew how to say "go potty" in Chinese.) If you want to use a customary family saying, or to make one up, by all means go ahead.

Some of us feel comfortable using *"Hurry up."* When your dog asks to be let out or when you take your puppy outside, say *"Let's hurry up and go outside,"* (or to the paper, or wherever). When the puppy begins to eliminate, say *"Hurry up!"* (As far as we know this hasn't backfired as when *"Hurry up"* is also used following "get off the sofa.") Don't forget to praise the puppy whatever words you use.

"Go to Bed"

Many of my family's visitors, professed dog lovers all, object to sharing the couch with a pet, strenuously object to having it curl up at their feet, and certainly don't want it leaning against their legs. My mother, not a dog lover but at least amiably tolerant of our pets, taught every one of them, *"That's enough."* After they greeted her, sniffed around for a treat, and were just settling down to visit, she would draw her hand away and say, *"That's ENOUGH!"* They soon learned to go find some other feet to curl up around or they would be sent "to bed."

In my home, the dogs' beds are multiple. Our dogs could have a bed in several rooms. A rug next to a recliner, a crate in the laundry room, or a pillow in the living room corner. We point to the particular bed we would like to see them in at the time. When they are puppies, we carry them to their crate after saying *"Go to bed."* When we have company, while we eat, or whenever our pets are underfoot a quick *"Go to your bed"* allows them to remain in the room and be part of the family. Very few visitors object to the presence of a family dog resting quietly in a corner of the room.

"Shake Hands"

Tell your puppy *"Shake,"* then pick up his right paw and shake it. (Because studies show that the majority of dogs are what we would call right-handed and because most people expect a right-hand shake, teach the puppy to offer the right paw by not accepting a left paw offer. Say *"No!"* Don't touch the puppy's left paw, say *"Shake!"* again and lift the right paw if necessary.) If you have to pick up the paw, shake it and praise the puppy just as highly as if he had handed you the paw without help. Say *"Good puppy, Sandy, what a good puppy,"* or whatever affectionate line you feel comfortable with. Give the puppy half of a dog biscuit, a bite of cheese, or a bit of liver. Repeat this activity at various times through the week. Your bright-eyed puppy will learn quickly to raise his paw.

Correcting Bad Habits

Bad habits, once established, are hard to break. Without realizing it, you could even contribute to the problem if you fail to make clear to the dog what you are asking him to rectify. Certainly this is true if you correct long after the fact. The young puppy just can't figure out which of his actions upset you. Your best approach in puppyhood is prevention.

Usually, if the mischief occurred out of your sight or earlier in the day, you can do little to correct it. You can fuss, but it won't prevent a recurrence. Be on guard for a similar infraction when you are at home. When you see your pet get into mischief, use the opportunity to teach a lesson. Jump in right away with scoldings and discipline.

Chewing

Sometime around the third month of life a puppy's permanent teeth will begin to emerge. Most puppies are considerably bothered by this process, gnawing and gumming their way through your treasures. Because the teething process can last from 7 to 18 months, this discomfort bothers us as well.

Canine College: Agility Class.

Left to his own devices a teething puppy will chew on any comforting object—a table leg, the front steps, or the rungs of your grandmother's rocker.

1. The first time you catch your puppy chewing the back porch steps say *"No!"*

2. Next, move the puppy to a new location and quickly offer his favorite chew toy.

3. Return to the porch steps and sprinkle the site with hot pepper sauce or cayenne pepper or a commercially prepared bitter apple liquid just in case you are not around the next time the puppy gets the urge to gnaw wood.

Be observant. When your puppy tires of the chew toy he may bypass those now nasty-smelling porch steps and head for a tasty chair leg instead. Say *"No!"*, rap the puppy lightly under the chin this time, then move him to a new location and again offer a chew toy substitute.

Puppies aren't the sole culprits here. Older dogs will also chew because of boredom, anxiety, nutritional deficiency, or lack of exercise. The remedy is the same. Say *"No!"*, distract the dog, pepper the object, check his diet, and offer a chewable substitute.

Wooden objects are not the only objects a young dog may like to chew. A puppy, not realizing the sharpness of that new set of teeth, will nibble at your fingers or tug at your ankles when he gets excited. Don't allow this type of behavior! Those are your fingers, and the puppy will eventually bite down hard enough to draw blood on you or a guest.

Say *"No!"* and move your hand away. If the puppy continues nibbling, say *"No!"*, hold his mouth shut and—using one finger—lightly rap him under the chin or on the nose. Stop playing with the puppy. Pick him up and move him to another area. Give him something else to play with and leave him alone. In a few minutes, come back and praise the puppy for being good. Act as though you forgot all about the problem—the puppy has.

Biting

Your puppy may growl at you when you correct him. He may even snarl when you remove your shoes from his mouth. Accept none of this behavior. Don't forgive these incidents with the "He's just a puppy" balm. Correct and recondition your pet immediately.

Many family adult dogs will bite if provoked. A dog that has been trained to guard and protect property or people will bite if instructed to do so. A territorial family dog will bite strange people and other dogs because of possessiveness. A frightened dog will bite if he is in pain.

Warning: Some adult dogs with unchecked aggression will bite without provocation. These animals are a danger to society and a disgrace to their owners. Allowing such dogs to run loose is irresponsible because they can pose a serious threat to public safety; moreover their owners could be held ethically, morally, and financially liable for the consequences of their pet's behavior.

Jumping Up

If you do not wish your puppy to jump on your guests or on you unless commanded to do so, begin training early.

1. Call the puppy to you, stoop down, and love him.

2. Tell him what a good puppy he is.

3. Walk away.

4. Repeat the lesson each time your dog attempts a jump.

Some owners of smaller breeds train their pets to jump into their arms on command.

Unhappy with the prospect of a spring-loaded 50-pound (23-kg) dog landing unexpectedly, and aware that even the best-trained dogs can't tell the difference between good clothes and training clothes, some Springer owners teach their dogs a similar, less jubilant command: The dog learns to rise on command on his back legs, placing his paws on the owner's waist. The dog is then given a hearty ear and chin rub or a treat. With few exceptions, this command cures unexpected jumping because it keeps you in control. You, in effect, invite the dog up when you want him up.

Barking

Very few habits are as annoying as unrestrained barking. Dogs will bark at unusual noises, bark from loneliness, bark at a rising moon, and sometimes bark just from the sheer joy of joining a neighborhood chorus.

1. If you are at home, open the door and call *"No barking!"*

2. Call your pet to you and give him a pat and a hug for coming. Remember, don't discipline the dog when he comes to you because the canine mind will make the wrong association. "I was out having a lot of fun," he thinks, "but you called me so I quit what I was doing to come to you. Boy, were you in a bad mood! I'm not going to come so quickly next time!"

3. If your dog continues to bark and is annoying you and the neighborhood, be prepared with some annoying tricks of your own. Think of ways to startle the dog so that instead of receiving satisfaction from barking, he receives an unpleasant surprise.

4. If the dog is inside the house, and there is a door between you, try startling the dog by rapping sharply on the door every time the

noise starts. If your dog is out of doors barking at the neighborhood strays, open the door and call him to you. *"Sandy, come!"* Sometimes, your dog is barking on "automatic" and this distraction will work wonders. Pet him and put him back out again. You had to get up, but at least you went back to sleep.

5. If you are gone during the day and have close neighbors who (rightly) complain about your barking dog, the solution is more complicated. Try to determine the cause of the outbreak and eliminate it. If the barking is caused by the arrival of the postman or a delivery person, enlist the aid of the complaining neighbor.

6. Pretend to leave as usual and ask your neighbor to come up to the door as the delivery person does. When your dog barks, you appear and scold him. *"No barking!"* Several unpleasant surprises such as an unhappy master can distract even the most dedicated barker.

KEEPING YOUR SPRINGER HEALTHY

Your veterinarian will encourage you, as your pet's first line of defense, to be observant. You often will spot changes in behavior, eating habits, and activity levels before such abnormalities are apparent to others.

Be aware. If your Springer normally eats well, is frisky and playful one day and the next day seems listless, refuses food, or feels warm, for instance, you should be alert for trouble. If this unusual behavior continues for several days, or is accompanied by a personality change, obvious intestinal problems, or hair loss, seek professional help.

You will be asked several questions. Be prepared with the answers.

✔ Are your pet's vaccinations complete and current?

✔ Have you made a recent change in your pet's diet?

✔ Is there an ongoing parasite control program?

✔ Have you noticed a marked decrease (or increase) in appetite, activity, or body temperature?

✔ Do you have any suspicions as to the cause?

Pretty as a picture.

Your Pet and the Veterinarian

Free bulletins and brochures are available from your veterinarian covering every subject from house-training a new puppy to caring for an aging pet. Your veterinarian will be happy to share the latest research findings that will help keep your Springer happy and healthy well into advanced old age.

Preventive Medicine

Your veterinarian has access to vaccines and preventive treatments designed to build up your pet's natural immunity. Failure to take advantage of these health-enhancing regimes is unfair to your pet and often, as in the case of rabies vaccinations, illegal as well.

Vaccines help prevent deadly and debilitating illnesses that can spread quickly through a neighborhood if left unchecked. Usually underway by the time a puppy is six weeks old and continued until age sixteen weeks, the following vaccines commonly are known as puppy shots. No pet should be without them.

Puppy Shots

At age six to eight weeks your puppy will typically receive a DHLPPC shot, known as "six in one" that will immunize against six very common but potentially deadly diseases: canine distemper, canine hepatitis virus, leptospirosis, parainfluenza, parvo virus, and corona virus. Different veterinarians suggest somewhat different vaccination schedules often depending on location. Your veterinarian will decide on the best schedule for you, but the timing is often similar to the following:

✔ Age six weeks: DHLPPC
✔ Age 12 weeks: DHLPPC Booster
✔ Initial heartworm preventive (usually chewable)
✔ Age 16 weeks: DHLPPC Booster

Your dog's veterinarian will be its second best friend.

✔ Heartworm preventive (monthly thereafter)
✔ Age six months: Rabies (annually thereafter)

Canine Distemper

Canine distemper, which at first resembles a common cold, is a highly contagious disease most common in unvaccinated puppies during their first year of life. Distemper is the leading cause of infectious death in dogs. Consequently, most puppies are given their first distemper vaccination while still with their mother.

Symptoms of distemper include a watery discharge from the eyes (beginning as a thin fluid but in a few days turning to a thick, yellow consistency) and a dry, mucus-caked nose. The dog has a fever, shows loss of appetite, and is listless. By the time the dog evidences the typical epileptic-type seizures, treatment is ineffective.

Canine Hepatitis

An infectious disease that can spread to other dogs, canine hepatitis affects the liver, kidneys, and lining of the blood vessels.

In fatal form, the dog suddenly becomes ill showing symptoms of sudden pain and evidencing severe bloody diarrhea.

Kennel Cough

Kennel cough is a highly contagious disease that spreads rapidly through a group of dogs. The viruses and bacteria that cause kennel cough are repressed by the parainfluenza-Bordetella vaccine. Administered as part of an annual vaccination series, this vaccine is important for dogs living in groups and those that are exposed to others in show or hunting environments. Those infected, though seemingly cured, can later experience the aftereffect of chronic bronchitis.

Parvoviral Disease

Canine parvoviral disease is a relatively recent, highly contagious disease first observed in the United States in 1978. The virus is transmitted from one dog to another through contaminated urine and feces. The usual victims are puppies under the age of five months. Springers, as well as Rottweilers and Doberman Pinschers, are more likely than other breeds to develop severe complications if infected, making vaccination a must for these breeds.

Symptoms of parvoviral disease include depression, loss of appetite, vomiting, extreme pain, bloody diarrhea, and high fever. A second form of the disease seems to affect the puppy's heart muscles. An infected puppy will stop nursing, cry out, and gasp for breath. Death follows soon after.

A comforting nap.

Canine Coronaviral Gastroenteritis

This disease is characterized by the sudden onset of vomiting and persistent diarrhea. Although mortality rates for coronavirus are low, it is important that the coronavirus vaccine be included in the vaccination program for maximum immunity benefits.

Rabies

The rabies virus, deadly scourge of summer months, attacks its victim's brain. Rabies affects all warm-blooded animals, including fox, skunk, bat, and man. In some cases saliva can be infectious a week before any symptoms appear. A series of treatments has been developed for humans, but rabies is fatal to dogs.

If you should encounter an animal that you suspect is rabid, keep your distance and call the authorities. Don't kill the animal. Laboratory tests on a dead animal can be misleading.

Heartworm Preventives

Heartworms have been identified in all 50 states, but many parts of the country, particularly those southern and western states with hot, long summers, are prime breeding grounds. The mosquito-borne larvae burrow their way into the dog's system. Once established, a female heartworm can produce 10,000 young every 24 hours.

Symptoms of heartworm infection include an intolerance for exercise and a soft, dry cough. Although mild cases of heartworms can be successfully treated, the best treatment is prevention.

Heartworm preventives in monthly or daily doses are vital for dogs in infested areas. The monthly dose can include, depending on the product, a preventive for roundworms, hookworms, and whipworms, making a year-round program invaluable.

How You Can Help

You are your dog's best friend.

✔ Be observant of his appetite, his elimination schedules, his moods.

✔ Inspect him for fleas and ticks and take appropriate measures to eradicate them.

✔ Stay in touch with your veterinarian and discuss deviations from the norm before such deviations get out of hand. Your pet depends on you for his health.

Taking Your Springer's Temperature

You should know your dog's normal body temperature. A hand held to the dog's nose is not always as reliable as is commonly believed Although a cold, wet nose is one sign of good health, a dry nose is not in itself a sign of illness.

Your veterinarian will take your healthy pet's temperature during routine puppy-shot visits. Note the range. A healthy Springer usually registers around 101°F (38.3°C).

✔ Obtain a heavy-duty rectal thermometer. Shake it down to at least the 96°F (35.5°C) mark.

✔ Lubricate it well.

✔ Lift your dog's tail and, using a twisting motion, insert two-thirds of the thermometer into the anal canal.

✔ Remove, wipe clean, and read. A reading more than 2°F (1°C) above normal is considered too high.

Giving Medicine

Eventually, every pet owner must learn to administer medicine, vitamin supplements, or heartworm preventive. Some medications, such as the heartworm preventives, are apparently pretty tasty. Take advantage of this unexpected benefit when you can, because some medicines seem to be pretty foul-tasting.

The accepted procedure is to open your pet's mouth and place the pill at the back of the tongue. Hold the mouth shut and stroke the dog's throat. When you release your hand, if the dog licks his nose, he has swallowed the pill.

You might, however, take advantage of your dog's impulse to swallow his food whole. Tear off two small bits of cheese. Place the pill in one piece and roll both pieces into a ball. Call the dog to you. Command him to sit and offer the plain cheese ball first. Then offer the cheese-wrapped pill. Occasionally vary the treat either by offering the cheese-pill first or coating the pill with peanut butter instead of cheese.

One veterinarian suggests cutting a Fig Newton in half, pushing the pill in one half and feeding it to your Springer. The other half is for you.

The fact that a Springer's jaw has loose skin between the teeth and the lip can be used to your advantage when offering liquid medica-

Hold the dog's mouth closed and stroke its throat until it swallows.

tion. Again, tell your dog to sit. Using your fingers, pull out the dog's lower lip at the back of his mouth, near the jaw hinge. Pour the medicine into this "pocket," allowing it to dribble down between the teeth into the dog's throat.

Weighing Your Springer

A simple procedure like getting your dog on a scale can sometimes be not so simple. Dogs dislike unsteady, shifting ground, and the best dog will resist your best efforts. Your veterinarian is trained to out-maneuver your pet and has access to professional floor-scale equipment.

If you feel the need at home to know just how much weight Sandy has gained, you might try this:

✔ Step on the scale alone.
✔ Record your weight.
✔ Pick up your pet and step back on the scale.
✔ Make a note of the weight; then, when you subtract the first figure from the second, the difference in the two figures is your dog's weight.

Some Common and Not-So-Common Problems

By the time your pet is six weeks old you should have established a good relationship with your veterinarian. Immunization schedules and behavior problems should be discussed and solutions agreed on. Your veterinarian will be pleased to help you maintain your pet's health between scheduled visits. Call if you need advice.

Fleas

Fleas and ticks are the bane of summer for our dogs. Unless we intervene, our pets scratch

Out for a stroll.

and bite their way through a miserable July and August until we and they are frantic. In our efforts to help, we throw an avalanche of products at the flea: chemically treated collars, ultrasonic collars, medicated shampoos and dips, chemical spot-infusions, garlic, brewer's yeast, and herbal medications. The house is quiet for a while, our pet is comfortable, but all too soon the scratch is on again. What has happened?

Flea's life cycle: In order to treat these pesty critters successfully it is important to understand their life cycle.

Just kidding, I'm not cold.

A flea's life cycle consists of four stages: egg, larva, pupa, and adult. Your pest control efforts must seek out and demolish the flea at each stage or you have only temporarily delayed the cycle, not eliminated it.

Adult fleas live by feeding on blood. Once the flea has fed, it must continue taking regular blood feedings or it will die. If it leaves the host for any length of time it cannot survive. You can kill adult fleas with dips and powders. Your dog can literally scratch them off his body, but the problem is that the adult flea began producing eggs within two to three days after receiving the first blood meal. The flea can produce 40 to 50 eggs per day at its peak production, a rate that can continue for several months, and produce several hundred eggs over the insect's lifespan of six to twelve months. So, the fleas you killed today with an insecticidal dip were only 1 percent of the potential number of fleas in your dog's environment. A point to remember: For every flea you see, 100 more are in various stages of development or in hiding.

Once laid, the flea's tiny, white, oval eggs probably fell off your pet and landed on your sofa cushions, in his bedding, on your carpets, or in the yard. Two to twelve days later these eggs hatched into small, maggotlike larvae. The larvae formed pupae (cocoons) from which eventually emerged—you guessed it—adult fleas, hungry for a blood meal.

Flea control: The secret to flea control, therefore, is to treat the flea's environment at each of its four stages of development. Ask your veterinarian to recommend a product for your area and be prepared for a four-week eradication schedule.

• *Week one:* Wash your dog's bed. Vacuum the carpet, the furniture, and the drapes. When you are finished vacuuming, change vacuum bags. Burn or otherwise dispose of the old bag. Sprinkle or spray the recommended product around your dog's sleeping quarters and play yard. Shampoo your pet with a good flea shampoo. Pay particular attention to the dog's head, under his arms, and his anus.

• *Week two:* Wash your dog's bed. Vacuum as before. Don't forget to burn or otherwise dispose of the old bag. If you don't, fleas will hatch in the bag. Use the insecticide as recommended.

• *Week three:* Follow the same procedure as week one. Your dog will receive two shampoos during this four-week assault (weeks one and three). Make bathing times fun for the dog.

• *Week four:* Wash, vacuum, and spray as before. Be assured that, although this program is initially time consuming, it is effective for weeks, even months, provided no reinfestation is introduced. Unfortunately, you must be prepared to resume treatment at the first sign of an outbreak.

Ticks

If your dog spends a lot of time outside, you should schedule a thorough, daily tick inspection. Although all ticks are capable of transmitting disease, the deer tick in eastern and midwestern states and the Pacific Coast tick found in Washington, Oregon, and California cause the most problems. Lyme disease, named in 1975 for the Connecticut community that first brought it to our attention, is potentially fatal to humans.

Ticks attach to your dog to feed and mate. The female will settle anywhere on your dog, usually on his earflaps, around his neck, or between his toes, sometimes gorging until it is the size of a large gray pea.

Removing the tick: To remove the tick, douse it with an alcohol-drenched cotton swab. She should die within five or six minutes. Then, using tweezers, catch the tick as close to the dog's body as possible and pull steadily. When the tick is removed examine it to be sure the head was released intact. If the head is torn, go back and look for mouthparts that may not have been removed. Swab the spot with more alcohol, search for and remove the smaller male tick, which should be resting nearby.

Mange

Usually characterized by excessive hair loss, mange is caused by mites that live in the pores of the dog's skin, burrowing into the skin to lay eggs. There are two types of mange: demodectic and sarcoptic. Dogs with sarcoptic mange scratch and itch excessively. The ear tips are often affected; in fact, crusty ear tips and a musty body odor are prime symptoms. Sarcoptic mange is treated with an insecticidal dip.

Veterinarians suspect that the demodectic mange, usually seen in puppies three to nine months old, is caused by a lack of immune response that may be hereditary. The *Demodex canis* mite is present in many dogs but causes problems only for a few. Some untreated puppies make spontaneous recoveries as their immune systems mature. However, the difficulties of adolescence, a change in habits, or a move to a new location can bring on an attack. The disease is characterized by hair loss from the front legs and face of affected puppies. As it progresses, the hair loss becomes generalized over the entire body. Unlike sarcoptic mange, demodectic mange does not itch.

Allergies and Hot Spots

Dogs have allergies just as people do. A dog can be allergic to almost anything, sneezing and itching in response to seasonal cycles, his environment, or occasional unfortunate contacts. Allergies also may cause the painful, itching, weeping bare patches of skin known as "hot spots."

Your veterinarian can identify some of these causes of allergies by means of allergy testing and allergy shots. In addition, your veterinarian can suggest the proper hypoallergenic diet if necessary and can prescribe ointments and diet additives, many of which contain such anti-inflammatory agents as Omega 3 and Omega 6 that reduce itching by as much as 20 percent.

CHECKLIST

Causes of Allergies

If your dog itches and sneezes, consider some of these most common causes:

1. contact allergens such as insecticides, detergents, soaps, flea powders, flea collars, plastic or rubber food dishes, or outdoor carpet dyes

2. food allergens such as soy, beef, chicken, corn, wheat, egg whites, milk, and fish

3. inhaled allergens such as house dust, ragweed, tree pollens, wool, feathers, and molds.

Worms

Most puppies are born with roundworms. Conscientious breeders deworm each litter at two or three weeks of age and again at five or six weeks. Many adult dogs are subject to whipworms, hookworms, and tapeworms. Although the puppies develop a certain immunity once treated, some rural owners routinely deworm their adult dogs once a year.

Diarrhea and Vomiting

Debilitating to the dog and unpleasant for the owner, continuing, foul-smelling diarrhea is a problem that should be treated immediately. Occasional diarrhea can be caused by indiscreet eating. Garbage, milk, rich food, a change in diet, or toxic plants often have a laxative effect. A rule of thumb is, if your dog throws up once or twice or if he has an occasional soft stool, he probably is all right. Cut back on his food and offer only dry kibble until the problem clears. If vomiting or diarrhea persists, however, call your veterinarian.

Hereditary Problems

The typical English Springer matures into a well-adjusted, amiable, confident companion comfortable in his reputation as a healthy, genetically reliable breed. As with all breeds, however, the Springer has his share of inherited problems.

Aggression: One problem in particular, the dog's sudden, uncontrolled aggression, is commonly referred to as Rage syndrome. The Springer is one of several breeds in which the disorder has been recognized. Animal behaviorist Karen Overall, speaking before the Morris Animal Foundation, identified the typical "toggle-switch, on/off" behavior characterizing this aggression. "The dog will be uncontrollably aggressive—you could hit it over the head with a two-by-four and it wouldn't notice you were there," said Dr. Overall, a lecturer at Pennsylvania School of Veterinary Medicine, "and then it turns off just as suddenly."

Dr. Overall noted that although the disorder is "probably overdiagnosed and under-reported," she warned her audience that animals afflicted with this syndrome are "extremely, extremely dangerous." If you have reason to suspect your dog's behavior, contact your veterinarian immediately.

Dysplasia: Although fewer than 20 percent of English Springers tested by the Orthopedic Foundation for Animals evidenced genetically generated hip problems, some lines do carry a defective gene for dysplastic hips and elbows that if untreated cause great discomfort to the dog. Symptoms of dysplasia begin to show at about six months of age.

Anybody home?

Defective genes: Some lines carry the defective genes that cause PRA (progressive retinal atrophy, an eye problem that can lead to blindness), cutaneous asthenia (a connective tissue problem), fucosidosis (a neurological disease), and PFK (a hereditary enzyme deficiency of the blood). Ask your breeder and double-check with your veterinarian.

Emergencies

All pet owners should be aware of certain procedures that could make the difference between life and death of their pet. Primary among these are the sudden illnesses and traumas of poisons and fractures.

A strategically located home first aid kit for your pet will help you in the event of an emergency. It should contain the following:

✔ tweezers
✔ scissors
✔ rubbing alcohol
✔ moist towelettes
✔ cotton-tipped swabs
✔ 3-inch (7.6-cm) roller gauze
✔ 3 × 3-inch (7.6-cm) sterile gauze pads
✔ rectal thermometer
✔ hydrogen peroxide

Bleeding and Fractures

A broken leg is the most common fracture and one that must be handled with great care until professional help is available. Try to keep the dog calm. Your primary responsibility is to immobilize the affected limb. Bone grinding against muscle and tissue can be excruciating, so work carefully.

Poisoning, Bites, and Stings

Puppies are inquisitive creatures, biting and snapping randomly at insects, lizards, and assorted flying hazards. Although older dogs have learned through sad experience to keep away from wasps, snakes, and the like, the urge

SPRINGER SOUNDBITES

"I miss the wagging little tail,
I miss the plaintive, pleading wail,
I miss the wistful, loving glance,
I miss the circling, welcome dance."
Henry Willett, "In Memoriam"

to snap at that annoying sound is occasionally too much to resist. Likewise, the sweet taste of antifreeze, the aroma of arsenic in snail and slug bait, and the appealing odor of decayed food are sometimes irresistible. Cocoa hull, often sold as garden mulch, contains theobromine, which is toxic to dogs.

Here are some common items that can cause problems for your Springer if imbibed in sufficient quantities:

✔ chocolate
✔ onions
✔ "people" medicine (antihistamines, sleeping pills, blood pressure pills)
✔ houseplants (Japanese yew, diffenbachia, philodendron, poinsettia, chrysanthemums, pothos)
✔ outdoor shrubs (rhododendrons, oleanders, azaleas, wild cherry)
✔ zinc (from pennies or from the nuts and bolts of kennel crates)

The following rank among the deadliest combinations hazardous to your pet:

✔ rat poisons containing strychnine, sodium fluroacetate, or warfarin (the dead rodent itself is poisonous)
✔ phosphorous found in fireworks or matches
✔ corrosives in household cleaners
✔ fumes from gasoline, kerosene, and turpentine
✔ antifreeze in doses of 1/2 teaspoonful per pound of bodyweight
✔ lead from paint, plaster, and putty.

Although the majority of snakes are nonpoisonous and their bites nonfatal, all snakebites can be extremely painful. Because snakebites from one of the poisonous varieties can be treated with specific antivenins, it is important to kill and identify the snake.

Symptoms of poisoning: Some of the symptoms of poisoning are abdominal pain, panting, vomiting, excessive drooling, tremors, uncoordinated gait, convulsions, and coma. If you suspect your dog has been poisoned, call your veterinarian immediately.

The Older Springer

After the first few years of rambunctious puppyhood and rebellious adolescence, you and your dog will come to know each other well. Your Springer will hear your car long before it turns into the driveway; he will distinguish your step from all the others he hears, and he will seem to read your thoughts—especially when outings and food are involved. You will settle into comfortable habits, your friendship the closer with age. With good care and good luck our Springer companions will live with us for 12 years or more.

Life Expectancy

As a result of a series of studies on life expectancy, experts have revised their approximations of equivalent ages of dog and human. The old one-for-seven equivalency is no more: At one time we believed that a one-year-old dog was the same physical and mental age as a seven-year-old child, for instance, but later studies lead us to believe a one-year-old dog is more equivalent to a 15-year-old adolescent.

Signs of Aging

By the time your Springer is ten years old you will notice a change in his daily routines. He will nap more frequently, chase butterflies less often, be slower to rise, and be less flexible in his movements. As he ages, hardening of the arteries puts a burden on his heart. Cancer, heart disease, and kidney disease are his enemies. His coat will thin out, and damaged hair will regrow at a slower rate. He will be less surefooted and will not attempt climbs he once made so easily. You can help your old friend by following a few, simple rules:
✔ Feed him a diet with higher protein, lower fat, and higher fiber to discourage obesity.
✔ Encourage moderate amounts of daily exercise to help his joints remain flexible.
✔ Don't change his daily routine. Avoid unnecessary travel and unfamiliar sleeping arrangements.

Dog/Human Age Equivalents

Dog's Age	Human's Age
6 months	10 years
8 months	13 years
10 months	14 years
1 year	15 years
18 months	20 years
2 years	24 years
4 years	32 years
6 years	40 years
8 years	48 years
10 years	56 years
12 years	64 years
14 years	72 years
16 years	80 years
18 years	88 years
20 years	96 years
21 years	100 years

✔ Don't let your pet loose near traffic; hearing goes before sight and smell.
✔ Consider allowing him to leave this life with dignity.

Euthanasia

Often, an old dog, beset with age-related ill health, can find no relief from suffering; it is then time to say good-bye. Your veterinarian will know when that time has come. Modern drugs can help that end come swiftly and without pain.

In her novel *The Flowering*, Agnes Sligh Turnbull spoke for many: "Dogs' lives are too short. Their only fault, really."

Books

American Kennel Club. *The Complete Dog Book*. New York: Howell Book House, 1998.

Baer, Ted. *Communicating with Your Dog*, 2nd Edition. Hauppauge, NY: Barron's Educational Series, Inc., 1999.

Coile, Caroline. *Encyclopedia of Dog Breeds*, 2nd Edition. Hauppauge, NY: Barron's Educational Series, Inc., 2005.

Rice, Dan. *The Dog Handbook*. Hauppauge, NY: Barron's Educational Series, Inc., 1999.

Tennant, Colin. *Breaking Bad Habits in Dogs*. Hauppauge, NY: Barron's Educational Series, Inc., 2003.

Wrede, Barbara. *Civilizing Your Puppy*. Hauppauge, NY: Barron's Educational Series, Inc., 1992.

Associations

American Kennel Club
51 Madison Avenue
New York, NY 10010

Canadian Kennel Club
89 Skyway Avenue, Suite 100
Etobicoke, Ontario M9W 6R4
Canada

English Springer Spaniel Field Trial Association, Inc.
Marie Anderson, Corresponding Secretary
29512 47th Avenue S.
Auburn, WA 98001

United Kennel Club
100 East Kilgore Road
Kalamazoo, MI 49001-5598

Top dog.

Sitting pretty.

Home base!

I N D E X

About the Author

Tanya B. Ditto, an award-winning member of the Dog Writers Association of America, is the author of Barron's *Shar-Pei*. She lives in Gulf Breeze, Florida.

Acknowledgments

The English Springer Spaniel Breed Standard is reprinted with the kind permission of the English Springer Spaniel Club of America.

Photo Credits

Norvia Behling: 55, 75, 76, and 77; Kent Dannen: 8, 9, 10, 11, 12, 24, 28, 29, 30, 40, 41, 42, 43 (top), 44, 53, 54, 59, 61, 65, 67, 73, 74, 83, and 92 (left and right); Tara Darling: 2-3, 7, 14, 17, 25, 31, 32, 46, 48, 49, 58, 69, 70, 86, and 93; Pets by Paulette: 4, 5, 13, 15, 16, 18, 27, 36, 47, 62, 63, 81, and 89; and Connie Summers: 19, 21, 23, 26, 43 (bottom), 52, 56, 60, 80, and 85.

Important Note

This pet owner's manual tells the reader how to buy or adopt, and care for an English Springer Spaniel. The author and publisher consider it important to point out that the advice given in this book is meant primarily for normally developed dogs of excellent physical health and good character.

Anyone who adopts a fully grown dog should be aware that the animal has already formed its basic impressions of human beings. The new owner should watch the animal carefully, including its behavior toward humans, and should meet the previous owner.

Caution is further advised in the association of children with dogs, in meeting with other dogs, and in exercising the dog without proper safeguards.

Even well-behaved and carefully supervised dogs sometimes do damage to someone else's property or cause accidents. It is therefore in the owner's interest to be adequately insured against such eventualities, and we strongly urge all dog owners to purchase a liability policy that covers their dog(s).

Cover Photos

Tara Darling

All inquiries should be addressed to:
Barron's Educational Series, Inc.
250 Wireless Boulevard
Hauppauge, NY 11788
www.barronseduc.com

International Standard Book No. 0-7641-2856-6

Library of Congress Catalog Card No. 2004065776

Library of Congress Cataloging-in-Publication Data
Ditto, Tanya B.
English springer spaniels: everything about history, care, feeding, training, and health / Tanya B. Ditto ; full-color photographs, illustrations by Michele Earle-Bridges.
p. cm.
Includes bibliographical references and index.
ISBN 0-7641-2856-6 (alk. paper)
1. English springer spaniels. I. Title.

SF429.E7D57   2005
636.752'4—dc22   2004065776

Printed in China
9 8 7 6 5 4 3 2 1